HOT TRAFFIC

HOW TO START AN
ONLINE BUSINESS
WITH ZERO INVESTMENT

CONTAINS 100 CRUCIAL INSIDER TIPS!

ROBERT SABELSTROM

"Hot traffic" is a key term in online business referring to visitors at your website who are actually looking for what you are offering.

The opposite of "hot traffic" is "cold traffic," meaning traffic that you drive to your website with investment of time and money, but once on your website, the visitors will not generate any income for you.

Table of Contents

INTRODUCTION

What can I learn from this book?

My name is Robert Sabelstrom, I have more than ten years of experience in building successful online businesses, as an entrepreneur, consultant and investor. In this book I summarize the knowledge I have gained in the process of creating online companies from scratch. During this process I have made tons of mistakes. My intention here is to help you avoid making all these mistakes, saving plenty of time and money when you start your own online business. This will enable you to grow quicker, move in front of your competition, get better financial results and more peace of mind.

The content of this book is based on my personal "lessons learned," including:

- ✓ How I cut my Google AdWords budget by 50%, but still reached higher profits
- ✓ How I lost > $5000 in worthless clicks, before I discovered the pitfalls of Google Display Ads
- ✓ How I grew revenues by 300% in less than a year, by applying a scalable landing page structure
- ✓ How I reached Google top 10 organic search for all my strategic key words

✓ How I then lost 30% of the Google traffic in one day, and how this could have been avoided

✓ How I used testimonials and enriched content to improve the conversion rate, and hence profits by > 25%

✓ How I reached 15 000 likes on Facebook, and how I used that to drive sales and customer satisfaction

✓ How I was able to automatize and outsource 80% of all administration

✓ How I discovered a way to find, test and evaluate new online business concepts in less than 3 weeks

Through my experience I learned to think of online business as a "vehicle" that can be trimmed. In this book I share the most important (top 100) trimming methods with you.

While reading this book, you will acquire the most important skills you need to be successful in the creation of your <u>profitable</u> online business. In summary, you will learn how to:

✓ Discover numerous online business opportunities

✓ Evaluate which online business opportunity you should choose for your start-up

✓ Test the business concept in small scale, without investments

✓ Get paying customers to your website the first day you launch, with Search engine marketing

✓ Optimize the paid traffic, typically enabling 50% less cost compared to your competition

✓ Transform your optimized campaigns in Google AdWords to Bing/Yahoo in less than 1 hour

✓ Work with Search Engine Optimization techniques to reach top 10 position in Google for free

✓ Build traffic from sources other than search engines and harvest the dual benefits of this

✓ Design your website to maximize the conversion rate (% of visitors you actually make money on)

✓ Get the customers to come back to your site over and over again

✓ Mobilize your customer to recruit new customers for you

✓ Use free (or very cheap) tools to keep cost at extremely low levels

✓ Outsource Customer Service, IT, production and such to minimize both your cost and effort

✓ Grow your business into new customer segments, geographical markets, product offerings, etc.

This book is divided into 7 logical chapters:

✓ Chapter 1-3: How to generate traffic to your website

✓ Chapter 4: How to convert the traffic into paying customers

✓ Chapter 5: How to maximize the lifetime value of your customer base

✓ Chapter 6: How to minimize cost and effort

✓ Chapter 7: How to grow the business (once your core business concept is proven and optimized)

Who is this book for?

There are two key steps in creating a business:

1. Come up with a business idea
2. Execute the idea into a successful business

The first step, the Idea, is very exciting. However, its impact on your online business success is much smaller than we tend to think. According to another successful online entrepreneur, Derek Sivers says, "The most brilliant idea itself is worth $20." It's the execution that makes it worth $20,000,000[1].

I have created this book with this ratio in mind. I devoted a few paragraphs to the $20 part- the Idea. The rest of the book is devoted to the $20,000,000 part- the Execution.

The main target group for this book is people who are starting (or considering to start) an online business. This book contains the recipe I would have "killed for" to have in my hand when I started my own online business in 2005.

The secondary target group for this book are people who already manage an online business. The sections about choosing a business concept will be less relevant to people in this category, since the business is already established. However, each of the 100 practical tips are valid and can be used as a "check list" for ways to increase the profitability of the business.

The third target group is people working within a company with an established online sales channel, which is (partly) managed by a third party. This book can help you improve the understanding of what you are actually buying and how to avoid potential pitfalls.

About the author - How I started my first online business in 2005

After returning home from 5 months of backpacking in Southeast Asia, I could not forget the fantastic feeling I had when I tried surfing for the first time in Kuta beach in Bali. Being a student at the time, I saved up some of my very limited savings and started searching the Internet for places where I could learn to surf.

---

[1] https://sivers.org/multiply

I found many "surf camps" around the world that offered a package deal of accommodation, food and surf lessons. It suited me perfectly, and I signed up for one week surf camp on Lanzarote, one of the Canary Islands.

Booking this trip was a real hassle! The website of the surf camp was really crappy; likewise were the payment options and the information I received from the surf camp via e-mail.

When I arrived at the Lanzarote airport, I was waiting for someone from the surf camp to pick me up. I still remember the itching feeling that I had been fooled. I had sent a large deposit to a company which I had doubts even existed. However, eventually my escort arrived and brought me to the surf camp where I had a fantastic week. I developed my (very poor at that time) surfing skills a lot and met several new friends from all over the world, who were there for the same reason that I was.

During the week I got to know the surf camp manager, and I gave him constructive feedback about the whole booking process and how they needed to develop their website and payment options. The owner was an excellent surfer, but technology was not "his thing". He received the feedback with a sigh and told me, "Robert, look, these online things you mention are not so important to us. Look around you; we already have customers coming from all over the world, having a great time here".

The last day of my stay we spoke briefly again. He had probably felt the strong drive I for these ideas and he came up with a proposal. "Robert, you know we don't have so many customers from your country, Sweden. Maybe you want to be an agent for us and arrange some more Swedish customers? We will give you a commission."

On the plane back home I thought through the proposal I had received. Could it make sense? I made some "guesstimates" about how many people in Sweden could potentially be interested in going to this surf camp in Lanzarote, and how big a share of them I could capture. It did not make sense.

But then another thought struck me. What if I would not only offer one surf camp, but maybe ten or even twenty, and what if I focused on a global audience, instead of just the Swedish market?

One year later, my best friend Johan and I were crossing out bullets on a paper. The paper contained a list of business ideas we were considering to try out as entrepreneurs. The list was long and it took us some time to evaluate all the ideas. After intense discussions the only remaining word on the list was "surf camps".

We didn't think that the "surfing" business had the best business potential, but it seemed decent and doable. Most importantly, it was an idea which could be tested without any capital (we were basically broke) and with limited effort. Another point was that I had developed a maniac passion for surfing, and this business idea could get me closer to the waves.

We spent around five weeks that summer creating the first version of unitedsurfcamps.com, setting up a legal company, arranging bank accounts and a payment service provider. At that time we had no prior knowledge of web-programming; we just learnt through free tutorials online. We launched the site and bought some keyword exposure on Google AdWords.

After three days of impatient waiting we secured the first booking. The feeling was incredible, it worked!

During the last decade UnitedSurfCamps.com has been the leading provider in our niche, enabling thousands of people to learn to surf at the 25 surf camps we promote worldwide. The website has been completely rebuilt twice and does no longer contain any of the original code I once wrote.

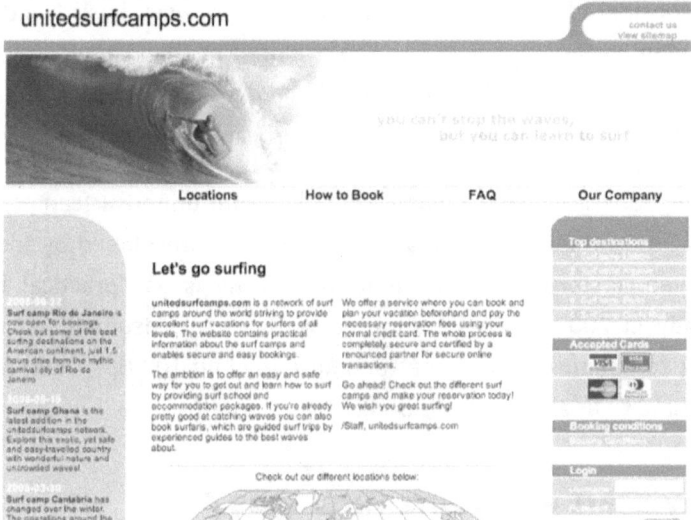

The above picture shows the first "home built" version of the website in 2005.

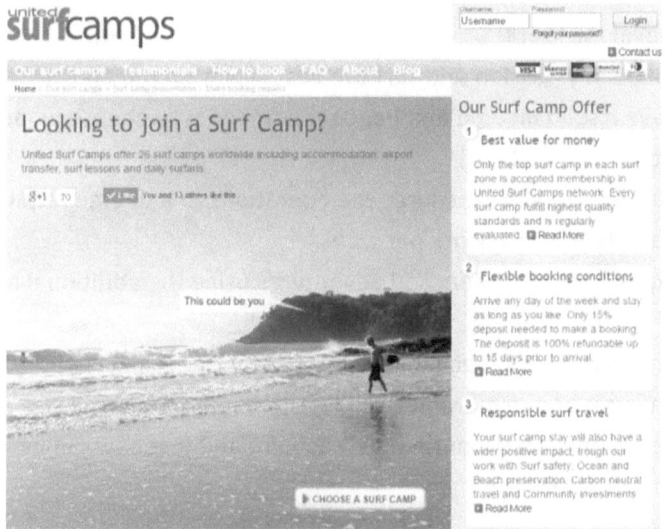

The above picture shows the v3.0 which is active since 2013.

During these ten years, I have reaped the benefits and joy of running an online business. We have sold surf trips for over $2,000,000 and are considered the leaders in our niche. However, both I and my founding partner, Johan, have also explored parallel careers and we (almost) always kept the promises we made to our spouses: "spend a maximum of 4 hours per week on the surf camp project."

In this book I will share many examples from unitedsurfcamps.com but also from other websites which have been developed by friends of mine. I started to document my learnings as "practical tips" already in 2007 when I started to work as a Consultant, advising other companies in these matters. Recently I hit 100 tips, and I felt it was time to finally write this book.

Why start an online business?

I'm happy that I made the decision to start my own online business. Thanks to this decision, and the effort that I put into this, I could:

- ✓ Travel the world
- ✓ Follow my passion and surf the best waves on the planet
- ✓ Have a solid income and hence the freedom to choose what I work with (and not)
- ✓ Automatize and outsource the operations to a degree requiring just a few hours' work per week
- ✓ Explore other careers and adventures using the additional hours of the week
- ✓ Understand the mechanics behind the great changes of the "information revolution"
- ✓ Be a pioneer and continuously acquire and test new online opportunities

✓   Help other companies to realize online business concepts

Starting an online business is an easy way to start your own business with limited investments. I began unitedsurfcamps.com just by "investing" five weeks one summer learning web programming with my friend. When you start an online business today, you can even skip this and instead start with ready templates in WordPress and focus on making money with the 100 practical tips I present in this book.

It is very rewarding to see how quickly you can change and grow an online business. I started unitedsurfcamps.com with just 3 surf camps. Then in less than one year, I was able to grow to over 20 surf camps and increase profits by over 300%. Doing the same in the "offline" world would require extreme efforts and investments.

If you already have a traditional sales channel, online is a quick way to drive new sales with very limited investments. It also provides superb data insights that can be used for the traditional sales channel.

Online Business models - How will I make money?

Despite my true passion for surfing, my goal with unitedsurfcamps.com was to earn money. I wanted it to be a "real deal" - my first, true business. Besides this, it doesn't matter how much you love the area that you choose to run your business. At some point it will become "just a job." So in the short-term, you may think that being an e-entrepreneur is just about "trying" or "having fun" or "the challenge." However, in the long-term, money is what makes any business sustainable. Besides that, you may also discover that money is actually a really good indicator of how good or how useful your business is to others.

In this book I will discuss:

✓   How to start generating revenue
✓   How to optimize it, so that you boost your profitability

Below, as an introduction I want to briefly discuss what online business models are currently available. There are basically four main ways to make money online:

1. Sell products or services - The most common model is usually referred to as e-commerce. However, e-commerce does not necessarily need to involve a physical product.
    Examples: *Shopify design awards!*[2] (Be inspired by the design of successful e-commerce sites using Shopify, one of the most popular e-commerce systems for small and medium -sized shops.)

2. Generate leads - This means that you have some interesting content driving visitors to your website. However, you do not "sell" anything directly to a visitor. Instead, you make money by referring the visitor onwards to another website that gives you a "kick-back" since you provided the "lead" to them. Either you have your own program, which is typically the case for large online newspapers, magazines and yellow-pages (but also some niches.) Or you are getting paid via an intermediary like Google AdSense or an affiliate marketing platform.
    Example: *SmartPassiveIncome*[3] (the author is open to opportunities in which he receives commission on these tools that he also recommends in the resources page.)

---

[2] shopify.com/design-awards
[3] smartpassiveincome.com/resources/

3. <u>Sell Premium content</u> - This is the model where you charge visitors to access part of the information you are offering. Examples of this are media consumption such as video, music, e-books, online software and membership platforms such as dating sites. Most often this is provided in a "Freemium model" meaning that part of the content is available for free. But if you want to consume more (once you are hooked) you need to upgrade to "premium" and pay a fee. Example: *I Will Teach You To Be Rich*[4] in which the author claims that he shares 98% of his knowledge for free. The rest is paid in the form of courses. Many apps for Smartphones/tablets are also based on this business model.

4. <u>Provide a marketplace</u> - In this model you provide an online location that will help match buyers and sellers of different products or services in an online environment. You can choose to make money only on the sellers, only on the buyers or both. Example: (*Airbnb.com*, global marketplace for short term rental of your home).

These four models can also be combined, but typically one model is the core concept and another one has been added to further optimize revenues.

When you are planning an online business, it is important that you conclude what will be your core revenue. If you are already running an online business, it is worth it to acknowledge which of those you are using. This will increase your awareness of the online business mechanics.

---

[4] iwillteachyoutoberich.com/products/

How do I choose the right online business idea?

This book is primarily about the execution and optimization of your online business. However, I have noticed, that coming up with an idea is also a challenge for beginning online entrepreneurs. Therefore, I briefly share my insights in the process of choosing the right online business idea below. If you already have an online business established, you may skip this section and move directly onto the next chapter.

The good news is that the online world is growing very fast. Therefore there is always an abundance of new ideas. If you apply lessons from this chapter, you will soon realize that the success factor is about concluding what NOT to choose, rather than how to come up with "the idea of the century."

Below I will briefly discuss:

✓ How to "discover" online business ideas
✓ How to evaluate them (in order to choose "the right" one)
✓ How to conceptualize the idea into a business plan

I see (at minimum) 7 principles as most important in how to "discover" online business ideas:

1. Offline→Online mind-set - Everything sold "offline" can be sold online. Literally everything! Examples include: Food & Other consumables; Clothes & Accessories; Advice (as e-books, trainings counselling); Bookings (at hotels, flights, restaurants, taxis, events, etc.)
   All the businesses above were traditionally sold offline only. Therefore, if you are looking for an idea for online business, see what's being sold offline and (still) not online in a competitive

way. If you can find a niche that is "hard to find locally" but still has enough demand for a bigger online market, you might have hit the "sweet spot." For example, an e-commerce business that focuses only on "Clothes from the 60s" or "professional dancing shoes" will most likely have an OK national demand but not have a local traditional shop in every town.

2. <u>Make it more convenient</u> - Think of finding information such as the price of a fridge 30 years ago. You would get in your car and drive the whole day to compare prices among local retailers. The same task now takes just five minutes. Providing accounting services as a company? Such work used to take 10 full-time employees, and now, just one location-independent person who could be, for example, in India can use online software to complete the same work. So in terms of convenience, Internet has changed "the game." Many online businesses are still being created around convenience. Hence, think how you can make the world a more convenient place.

3. <u>Make it cheaper</u> - Let's take a traditional, offline business. It sells electronics. It has 10 retail stores and 40 employees. It rents an inventory warehouse. It owns stock. It has trucks.
Now, imagine you could reach all those clients without 40 employees, without your own trucks, without the retail stores, even without the stock (in a drop shipping model, discussed in Tip #83.) There are still many niches around in which the "online price pressure" position is open.

4. <u>Come in as a 2nd or 3rd player and dominate the market</u> - There is a common view that the first company to discover (or enter) a market niche dominates it. However, this is often untrue. Companies, that enter first, make the most mistakes and pay a premium for educating their market. It is often the 2nd or 3rd company in the market that succeeds. Examples include even multimillion dollar companies like Facebook and Google.

5. <u>Immature niches</u> - This was the case with unitedsurfcamps.com. Even though online business had come a long way in the general travel industry, it was still lagging in the surf niche when we started. A more recent example of mine is a company I supported with an online concept for car recycling in Poland, which in 2014 still had zero "online" competition.

6. <u>Follow your passion</u> - Another dimension is to ask yourself what you are passionate about? My passion is surfing, so I naturally started an online business in the surfing industry. This gave great "fuel" to the business development and made it easier to become an "expert" in my niche.

7. <u>Think about your unsatisfied needs</u> - Have you ever been struck with a thought like: "Wouldn't it be great if...?" This is an indication that you have a new business opportunity within your grasp. Continue that thought and think how it can be conceptualized into a business.

Following one or a few of these principles, you will begin to discover many ideas. To me it happens quite often, but only in the latest years I have developed the discipline to also write them down in a list.

To make a first evaluation of your business ideas, I suggest considering the following key criteria:

1. <u>Market niche attractiveness</u> - How much money will I make if I am successful?
   - ✓ Market size
   - ✓ Market growth
   - ✓ Regulatory framework
   - ✓ New trends affecting the market

2. <u>Ability to capture the market</u> - How probable is it that I will succeed?
   - ✓ How strong is the competition in the niche?

     ✓   Do I have any prior knowledge and experience of the niche?

     ✓   Am I, or can I see myself becoming passionate about this?

3.   <u>Risk</u> - How much resources do I need to put in to test the idea?

     ✓   How much time and effort will it take to test the idea?

     ✓   How much money do I need to invest up front?

     ✓   Other risks?

A quick way to evaluate the first point - market niche attractiveness - is to start using the keyword planning tool in <u>Google Adwords</u>. Here you will be able to see the monthly search volumes for the strategic keywords associated with your business idea.

The keyword tool in Google Adwords will also be helpful to evaluate how strong the competition is in this niche.

Keyword (by relevance)	Avg. monthly searches ? Jun 2014	Competition ?
surf camp	8,100	High
surf school	3,600	Medium
learn to surf	1,900	Low
surf lesson	390	Low
surf holiday	320	High
surf resort	210	Medium
surf vacation	140	High

As indicated in the picture above, my chosen niche "surf camp" has today high competition in paid ads, meaning that many companies are paying to be associated with this search term. While a business focused more on "surf school" and "learn to surf" is less competitive, it still has a decent demand. After reading the next chapter in this book, you will have all the insights you need to master Google AdWords.

Just note that the monthly search volume estimates are dependent on the period you choose for the data extraction. It is crucial to understand also the seasonal effect and how much the market is growing/declining year by year. The best tool to analyze this is Google Trends.

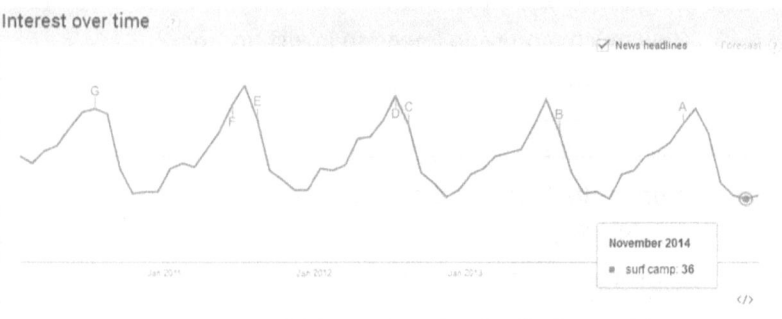

As shown in the picture above, the search term "surf camp" is very seasonal and during November, it only generates 36% traffic volumes compared to the highest month (June). Hence, if you estimate the market size using Google AdWords during the month of June you need to keep this in mind, not to overestimate the market size.

In the picture above, you can also note a somewhat declining demand; every year the peak is little smaller. Even though it is just a few percentage points of decline per year, it would, of course, be more attractive with a positive growth.

Another indication of how strong is the competition is their Page Rank. This is a scale of 1-10 showing how strong a website is in organic search (further discussed in chapter 2.) As a rule of thumb, I would say that if you find more than four competitors that have higher page rank than "4," it will be tough to compete in this niche for those who start up from scratch.

However, the most important research activity is to evaluate the competition's presence online. I suggest you go through all companies that are listed on the first page in Google when you search for key words associated with the niche you evaluate. There will always be competitors and new entrants because the Internet has low barriers, but you need to ask yourself, "What can be done smarter?" For example, can you differentiate from your competitors by:

- ✓ Making a simpler (not as messy) website, for example, by targeting a narrower niche?
- ✓ Creating a more trustworthy website?
- ✓ Creating a more enthusiastic website?
- ✓ Creating a better mobile/ tablet website or application?
- ✓ Competing in the areas of better convenience in service, customization, payment options, etc.?
- ✓ Competing on better prices?
- ✓ Other?

The third of the main points for evaluating an online business idea is the risk, meaning how much money, time and effort you need to put into testing your idea. The risk level will mainly be determined by how you plan to differentiate your business and what you are selling (e.g., physical products vs. leads.) After reading chapter 6 of this book, you will know all the "best practices" to minimize the costs and effort, both in the start-up phase and over time.

After comparing a few different business ideas with the criteria suggested above, you will get a good feeling of how attractive they seem in relation to each other. Once you have chosen an idea, the next step is to get a simple business plan down on paper.

Here is a structure I usually use:

1. A short description of the business idea - Use the "elevator pitch" concept, meaning that if you meet a potential investor in

the elevator, you should be able to pitch the idea clearly and in an inspiring way before the elevator ride is over.

2. Traffic generation - Describe how you will get visitors to your website, following chapter 1, 2 and 3 in this book

3. Business model - Describe how you will be able to monetize this traffic over time, using chapter 4 and 5 in this book.

4. Operations - How will you run the company? Use some of the best practices in chapter 6 of this book

5. Long term strategy - What is the long-term growth plan if the concept is successful?
Which of the dimensions in chapter 7 will be the second and third step of your business?

6. Business case - Financial simulation of revenues and costs over time.
How much money can you make (in a high vs. low scenario) based on the market size and competition in the niche? How much do you need to invest and what is the return on investment? Typically, the easiest tool to use for this task is Excel.

7. Roll-out plan -What will you do? In what order? With which deadlines? Show all the activities needed to launch the business. Set a clear action list with a responsible person. Set some main "milestones" A good example is a beta launch of the site for friends and family to discover the first transaction expected, etc.

Once you have this business plan documented (typically in 5-10 pages using Word or PowerPoint), you can use it to get feedback from friends and experts. Then it's time to make the go/no go decision, meaning if it is worth to test the model in its simplest format, or not.

Resources mentioned in the Introduction

✓ **WordPress** (wordpress.com) - Great platform to build your own webpage with no coding or designer skills using paid or free templates.

✓ **Google AdWords** (google.com/adwords) - Platform for buying search traffic. Contains a keyword planner tool that gives you great insights in choosing the "right" business idea.

✓ **Google Trends** (google.com/trends) - Service in which you can see popularity of a search phrase over time. You can also compare two or more search phrases in terms of search volume.

✓ **Check Page Rank** (checkpagerank.net) - Service that lets you check your competitors' page ranks.

CHAPTER 1

Optimize Paid search traffic

The first three chapters of this book cover the key success factors to get potential customers to visit your website. In online business this is commonly referred to as "traffic" and can be divided into three main groups with different logic outlooks:

1. Paid search traffic
2. Organic search traffic
3. Other (not search) traffic

We will start with the first group, Paid search traffic!

Introduction - What is Paid search traffic?

If you are looking for the answer to a question, what do you do? You google it! If the question you ask yourself connects to a potential purchase of a product or a service, then you are a potential buyer for an e-commerce site.

Let's say you have heard it is possible to design and order a tailor-made shirt online at a much lower price than by ordering locally in person from a tailor. You would probably google something like "tailor made shirts", "tailor fit shirts," "tailored shirts," or something similar. This is what Google will then show:

There are about two million web pages that refer to "tailor made shirts," but the only ones that count are the ones that show up on Google's first page = the Top10 results. The reason for this is that >90% of all people who search do not visit the second page (positions 11+) on Google[5]. That's why all the companies try to get (and stay) on the first page of Google search results.

However, the "Top10" phrase is not fully correct, since it only refers to the <u>Organic search results</u>. (I will explain what "organic search" means and how it works in chapter 2.) Above and to the right of the organic search results, Google shows the <u>Paid search results</u>, meaning paid ads in a similar format as the organic search results constructed within the Google AdWords program.

This Paid Search traffic is often referred to as "Search Engine Marketing" (SEM) while the techniques to rank high in the organic

---

[5] chitika.com/google-positioning-value

(not paid) search are referred to as "Search Engine Optimization" (SEO.)

Paid Search traffic actually stands for 96% of Google's income[6] and is used by 1.2 million website owners worldwide[7]. The services are so popular among business owners, because:

✓ You can measure results of every penny
✓ When properly done, it's inexpensive
✓ No entry barriers (with as low as a $1 budget) and gain customers the first day

It basically works like this:

1. Go to adwords.google.com and create an account.
2. Start a new campaign and decide which demographic parameters to target (e.g., which city/country, mobile/pad/computers.)
3. Decide which keywords such as "tailor made shirts" and "tailored shirts" you want to target.
4. Decide how the ad (meaning the "inorganic search result") should look when somebody searches for your chosen keywords.
5. Decide a maximum cost per click (e.g., $0.10) you are willing to pay for each click on the ad.
6. Decide the maximum daily budget (e.g., $10/day) you are willing to pay for the campaign.

How often and in which position your ad will show depend on two main things:

---

[6] investopedia.com/stock-analysis/2012/what-does-google-actually-make-money-from-goog1121.aspx
[7] wordstream.com/blog/ws/2012/08/13/google-adwords-facts

1. The <u>quality score</u> of a chosen keyword. This is a scale of 1-10 of how relevant your website is in relation to the chosen keyword. For example, if you have chosen the keyword "tailor-made shirts," but the ad is directed to a website which is selling dog food, your quality score will be low (further discussed later.)
2. Your maximum <u>cost per click</u>. Your bid, meaning how much you are willing to pay for each click on your ad and from there, the click directs the visitor to your website.

Google AdWords works like an online auction. Every time somebody places a search query, Google ranks all websites that have placed a bid on this keyword. Assuming that all quality scores are the same, the one who has placed the highest bid will be listed at the top of the inorganic search results. But in case one bidder has a much higher quality score, he can still rank higher even while paying less for a click.

The above section was a very brief description of Search Engine Marketing fundamentals. Once you learn how to use Google AdWords effectively, you will be able to generate inexpensive, well targeted and fully measurable traffic. However, if you do it randomly, you can easily "burn" big budgets, attracting inappropriate traffic that will not bring you any income. The remaining part of this chapter will cover the most important pitfalls and best practices of how to effectively manage and optimize your benefits in relation to cost and time from paid search traffic.

If you are not familiar with Google AdWords at all, I strongly recommend that you spend approximately one hour studying the "How it works" section at <u>adwords.google.com</u> (which is superb!) This way you will benefit much more from the remaining part of this chapter.

Keyword knowledge is king

Paid search traffic is the quickest way to generate "hot traffic" to your website. "Hot traffic" means visitors who are actually looking for what you are selling. The opposite of "hot traffic" is "cold traffic," meaning visitors that click on your ad (which you will pay for) but once they arrive on your website, they will not generate any income for you.

When someone searches for "surf Portugal," we do not know if he is looking for travel tips for surfing, surf school, or surf board rental? We can't even be sure if he is looking for wind surfing, kite surfing or surfing (wave riding), or maybe something completely different? If he, on the other hand, is searching for "surf camp Portugal," it is more likely that he is to be considered as a potential customer ("hot traffic") for unitedsurfcamps.com.

It hence makes sense to target niche key words like "surf camp Portugal" rather than broad keywords like "Surf Portugal."

So what is the implication if I instead target broad keywords?

1. Bidding for the keyword "surf" or "surfing" would cost a lot of money per click since you would compete with everyone bidding for combinations of "surf+."
2. This would also generate a lot of cold traffic (many irrelevant clicks.)
3. Consequently, this would turn into a high cost (or at least quick depletion of your daily AdWords' budget) without much income.

So the first argument to use niche keywords, for example, "surf camp Portugal" rather than broad keywords such as "surf Portugal" **is the "hot traffic" they generate**. The other argument is **lower cost per click**, since the competition is typically higher (driving up the bids) for broad keywords. If bidding for "surf Portugal," your bid will be compared to other bidders' advertising surf boards, surf forecasts and surf + and not only "surf camps."

Based on the above, it's time to declare my first tip:

Tip #1: Use "niche" rather than broad keywords

Ok, this sounds simple, but how do I figure out which are my best niche keywords?

To be successful in using Paid search traffic, you need to maximize the hot traffic while minimizing the cold traffic, and the first step to master this is to really, profoundly understand what keywords potential customers (= hot traffic) are using, or not using.

The most effective way to do this effectively is to generate a long list of keyword combinations and then to analyze them both from "market size" (how often the keyword is searched for) and "competition" (how many others bid on the keyword and what they are willing to pay.) I recommend a simple three step approach to generate your first list of qualitative keywords:

1. Brainstorm and write down keywords by "thinking like your potential customer."
2. Run this first list of keywords in the Keyword planner tool which is available via your Google AdWords' account. (It takes less than 10 minutes to start an account.) The tool will both generate ideas for similar keywords (to add to the list) as well as give real insight of market size and competition.
3. Search each keyword in Google to see who else is bidding for these keywords and who is ranking high organically (discussed in Chapter 2.)

While applying the third point of this analysis, you will get a good feeling around what really are relevant keywords for you and who are your potential competitors and not. You can also use KeywordSpy or similar tools to do this faster. In a smaller scale, it is available free of charge.

Tip #2: Benchmark competitors' keywords

It is not so important that you nail all the keywords to 100% from the start. The point is to start with a few keywords and then update the list based on the knowledge you get from running the campaigns. Google will even give you suggestions on which keywords to add to your campaign as they are running.

One very important outcome from the above approach is that you will conclude which are your most strategic keywords. In other words, this process will provide the keywords that can generate the most traffic to your website. These strategic keywords you also want to target in the Organic search (discussed in chapter 2.)

When you have tested your keywords for a few weeks, each search term can be further optimized by using "match types." Here is the example from Google AdWords' support pages that visualize this:

Match type	Special symbol	Example keyword	Ads may show on searches that	Example searches
Broad match	none	women's hats	include misspellings, synonyms, related searches, and other relevant variations	buy ladies hats
Broad match modifier	+keyword	+women's +hats	contain the modified term (or close variations, but not synonyms), in any order	hats for women
Phrase match	"keyword"	"women's hats"	are a phrase, and close variations of that phrase	buy women's hats
Exact match	[keyword]	[women's hats]	are an exact term and close variations of that exact term	women's hats
Negative match	-keyword	-women	are searches without the term	baseball hats

33

The main reason to use match types is to:

✓ Frame your potential audience
✓ Make sure your ad is primarily being shown to potential customers (hot traffic!)

For example, a user searching for "wind surf camp" would not be relevant for unitedsurfcamps.com that only caters to "wave-riding surfers;" hence, the "-wind" can be included as a negative keyword.

Neither would someone searching for "camp sites Portugal" be a potential customer, but he would trigger an ad with the keyword "surf camp Portugal." By rephrasing the keyword to "+surf camp Portugal the ad will only show if the user is including "surf" as part of the search query.

Tip #3: Use "match types" to avoid cold traffic

If you sell several products or services in different categories and maybe on different markets, you will quickly end up with thousands of keywords to target. The only way to manage this is to evaluate and apply a logical campaign structure.

Google AdWords basically has five levels of structure:

1. Account level - Highest level where you have unique log-in details and billing information.
2. Campaign level - First grouping where you set a daily budget such as $10/day; geographic targeting (e.g., "UK + USA" or "50 km radius around Paris") and language targeting, for example, English speaking users only. Here you also choose if the campaign shall be active only for search network or also for display network (discussed in Tip #9 and #37.)

3. Ad group level - An ad group contains one or more ads and a set of related keywords. Typically you would group all the ads and keywords in this ad group on one product or service.

4. Ad level - The advertisement that shows when somebody searches for your chosen keywords. Typically you start with one ad per ad group before testing more variants (discussed in tip #5.)

5. Keyword level - The lowest level where you might end up with thousands of keywords after accumulating all running ads. Note that the same keyword can appear in different ads, ad groups and campaigns (depending on how you have split your account).

In the unitedsurfcamps.com example, there are 25 different surf camps marketed around the world. This calls for using 25 ad groups. One ad group focuses on Surf Camp Santander (located in Northern Spain) and only contains keywords connected to this geographic area. Some examples are "Surf camp Santander," "Surf school Santander," "Surf holiday Santander," "Surf camp Cantabria," "surf camp Spain," etc.)

Each of these 25 surf camps has its own landing page (discussed in Tip #24 and #48.) An example is unitedsurfcamps.com/surf-camp/Santander where only traffic related to surfing in Santander/Spain should land.

If a user is searching only for "surf camps", "surf camps in Europe" or "cheap surf camp deals," I want him to end up on a more general landing page (unitedsurfcamps.com/our-surf-camps). This could be managed by creating additional ad groups, but since you might want to have a different budget and audience for these broader keywords, I have set it up as its own campaign called "general search terms."

Further on, when starting unitedsurfcamps.com in 2005, we soon discovered that our main search term "surf camp" meant something different in USA compared to Europe. In USA, it is mainly used to describe kids' summer camps (with a surfing theme) which are completely different from Europe where surf camps are mainly focused on adults. Hence, we put the USA market in a separate campaign and adapted the marketing message with "surf vacation" instead of "surf camp" and quoted all prices in USD instead of EUR, specifically for users from USA. This enabled us to block a lot of cold traffic (parents looking for kids' summer camps) and attract more hot traffic from this specific market.

Hence, the campaign structure of unitedsurfcamps.com ended up as follows:

1. General keywords (5 ad groups: Surf camp, Surf holiday, Surf vacation, Surf trips, Surf travel)
2. Europe (25 ad groups: Surf camp Santander, Surf camp Lisbon, Surf camp Ireland...)
3. USA (25 ad groups: Surf vacation Santander, Surf vacation Lisbon, Surf vacation Ireland...)

<u>Tip #4: Carefully evaluate the best campaign structure</u>

Find more tips about how to effectively structure your account via AdWords' support pages. The key success factor is to really think this through and adapt what is most logical for your specific market and product, before launching thousands of keywords.

Optimize the ad design

When managing your keywords effectively, you enable your ads to show up with the right search queries for the right audience. The next step is to make that audience click on your ad (given that they are potential customers = hot traffic) and come to your landing page where they can make a <u>conversion</u>, which means generate income for you (further discussed in chapter 4.)

The key question is: How to write the optimal text ad?

The answer: You don't need to know how!

You can apply a simple "trial and error" technique called <u>A/B-tests</u>. Since Google AdWords enable you to have several ads connected to the same Ad Group you can:

1. Make two ads with different features (which would be split 50/50) for the users who see the ad.
2. Then you can compare which ad has the highest performance, for example, measured as the <u>CTR = "Click through rate"</u> or in other words, how many times the ad was clicked in relation to how often it was displayed.)

I.e., when I tested the following two examples for unitedsurfcamps.com it was clear which one to use:

#	Ad	CTR
A	Surf Camps unitedsurfcamps.com Surf Trips, Surf School & Lodging Selection of 25 surf camps worldwide	2.24%
B	Book a surf camp online unitedsurfcamps.com Surf Trips, Surf School & Lodging Selection of 25 surf camps worldwide	1.68%

Variant A actually generates 2.24/1.68 -1 =33% more traffic to the website than Option B

Tip #5: Use A/B test to optimize the ad appearance

Note that it is key to have a hypothesis of what to test and to test one feature at a time. (In the example above, we tested only the headline.) If you test too many changes in the ad at the same time, you will not know which component is connected with what improvement. Once you pick a winner in your first test, you can go on to test another thing and keep iterating until you have optimized to the max.

How you design your ad will not only have effect on the CTR (click through rate,) but it might also affect the quality score. Quality Score is an estimate of how relevant the ad is in relation to the chosen keywords and landing page. As discussed previously, having a higher quality score is very attractive as it typically leads to lower cost per click and better ad positions. Quality score can be improved by three main drivers:

1. Improved CTR - Which the A/B test above will achieve. A high CTR tells Google that the users are interested in your ad (since they click on it) and hence, it is relevant and deserves a higher score.
2. Keyword consistency in the ad text - Having the same keyword in the ad text that you have chosen for the ad group shows Google that the keyword is relevant for you and hence deserves a higher score.
3. Keyword consistency on the landing page - If the keyword in the ad text also appears frequently on your landing page, this shows Google that the users are being sent to the "right place" and hence deserve higher score.

Just note that point 2 and 3 above calls for a "trade-off" since the implication of optimizing them fully means you should have an endless number of ad groups and landing pages (one for each niche keyword.) This is not a viable strategy from operations' point of view and hence needs to be balanced.

The success factor is to conclude what your most <u>strategic keywords</u> are and then use specific ads and landing pages for each strategic keyword.

Tip #6: Create separate ads and landing pages for each strategic keyword

How many landing pages you use and how you connect them via links are also key success factors for Organic search traffic. In the next chapter, this will be discussed in detail.

Click through rate (CTR) does not tell the whole story. It merely shows how much traffic comes to your site in relation to how often your ad is shown. It does not tell whether this traffic actually converts into an income for you. The good news is that this can easily be tracked! Insert a few lines of code provided by Google AdWords on your landing pages, and you will be able to see which traffic actually converted, (e.g., made a booking, purchased a product or anything similar.)

This enables you to follow up with some useful metrics (per ad, ad group, keyword, etc.)

1. <u>Click conversion rate</u> = What is the percentage of clicks that actually generates a conversion
2. <u>Cost/ conversation</u> = Total ad cost divided by the number of conversions
3. <u>Return on Marketing</u> = Generated income/ total ad cost

By focusing on conversion rates, not only clicks, you get the full picture and can compare how much money you actually spend to generate each sale.

Let's go through a small exercise to exemplify this:

1. Let's say you are selling product online for $30.
2. Your direct cost to buy or produce for this product is $12.
3. This means that for each sale of this product, you get a "gross margin" of 30 - 12 = $18.
4. You use Google AdWords to get traffic to the site where you sell this product and your average cost per click (CPC) is $0.10. (It does not sound like much, right?)
5. Competition gets harder and you raise the bid to $0.20, still not so much?
6. But if only 1% of the users that click on your ad actually complete the desired action, your cost per conversion would go from (0,10/ 0,01 =) $10 to (0,20/0,01=) $20 per conversion.
7. Since your gross margin per product is $18, the conclusion is that instead of making 18 - 10 = $8 per conversion, you are now losing 18 - 20 = -$2 per conversion.

Tip #7: Track and focus on conversions (not only clicks)

By reversing the example above, you can also calculate your maximum cost per click:

1. Your gross margin per product is $18.
2. Now, the maximum cost per conversion you could accept is $18. (Otherwise, the sale will be negative.)
3. Your conversion rate is 1% (meaning that 1 out of 100 clicks actually buys your product.)
4. This means that your maximum cost per click is 18 x 0.01 = $0.18.

5. Note that this is the maximum. Ideally you want to spend much less so you can get the healthiest margins on each conversion to cover your other costs.

One way to improve the conversion rate is to use ad extensions to guide the user and lead him closer to a desired action. There are five main types of ad extensions:

1. Sitelink extensions - Show additional links to subpages of your website which the user can click directly on, such as "Our products," "How it works," and "Contact us."
2. Location extensions - Show a pin with Google maps where your business is located (especially useful with local mobile searches with a plan to visit you physically.)
3. Call extensions - Enable the user to click a button to give you a phone call directly.
4. App extensions - Show mobile and tablet users a link below your ad text that sends them directly to the app store to download your app (if that is what you are selling.)
5. Rating and review extensions - Show the users what quantitative (e.g., 4.5/5) or qualitative testimonials are available such as "great experience, I will be back" from current and previous customers.

Tip #8: Use ad extensions to facilitate conversions

Different ad extensions obviously work best for different types of business models and situations, but most likely at least one of the above will be attractive for you to experiment with.

Successful bidding strategies

The goal of using Google AdWords is to maximize the net profit by generating as much "hot traffic" as possible with as little advertising cost and time management as possible. This trade-off can, to a big extent, be affected by external factors, such as bid competition of different search terms, user behavior (if somebody searches for the term or not) and changes made by Google. But there are also several factors you can influence by applying a solid bid strategy and thereby, avoid costly mistakes.

One of the most common pitfalls in my experience is when people who are new to AdWords start using both Search and <u>Display network</u> marketing. "Display network" means your ad will show up on various websites that are affiliated with <u>Google AdSense</u> that have a completely different logic (further discussed in chapter 3.) Using combined Search and Display targeting is the default setting in Google AdWords, so you need to actively choose "Search Network only" for each campaign to avoid the described issue.

So what is the problem with Display network marketing? The problem is that if you are not using very specific techniques (further discussed in Tip #37), the Display network will most likely eat up all your daily marketing budget and stop your ads from showing up for real potential customers who search for your services on Google. The reason is that there are lots of scam sites being created solely to drive people to click on Google AdSense links. Further on, if you do actually get a real potential customer to click on a display network ad, they are probably "less hot" than somebody who actively searches for your product or service on Google and you would hence want to pay less per click.

Tip #9: Focus on real Search traffic - avoid Display network marketing in the start-up

Just note that I only recommend you to avoid Display network in the start-up, meaning the first few months when you optimize your Paid search traffic. Once you have this under control, you can experiment with Display Ads in a very cautious way which I explain in detail under tip# 37 in chapter 3.

A great feature in Google AdWords (both for Search and Display marketing) is Remarketing campaigns. This means that you make targeted ads to people who have already visited your website and "window shopped." If you can get them back in the store, they are probably more likely to convert than the average visitors.

Tip #10: Experiment with Remarketing campaigns

Technically, Remarketing campaigns work just like conversion tracking. You add short snippets of codes on your landing pages, and Google will then know if somebody who searches for your chosen keywords has been your site before. You can then reach this specific target group with additional keywords, adjusted bids (affecting the position and CTR) and decide to activate the display network only for these users (avoiding the typical pitfalls of Display networks.) You can also adjust the ad design and write a specific message (e.g., special promotions/ "Call to actions") that is only visible to them.

There are many blogs online that explain the mechanics and techniques of remarketing in more detail. For further reading, please see the footnote[8].

---

[8] blastam.com/blog/index.php/2013/04/google-remarketing-boosts-conversion

Besides optimizing the financial effect of using Google AdWords, you also have your own time and effort to consider. One of the best developments available by Google in my opinion is the "automatic rules" function. Basically, there are five main automatic rules you can activate:

1. Change daily budget when...
2. Pause campaigns when...
3. Enable campaigns when...
4. Send email when...
5. Create rule for ad groups, keywords or ads

Personally, I have had great success in the creation of specific rules regarding the <u>bid for each keyword</u>. By tracking the actual cost per conversion, not only cost per click, I discovered that a viable bidding strategy for unitedsurfcamps.com is to be in the <u>third position</u> of the inorganic search result.

The reason for not being in the top 1 or 2 is that you then tend to get many clicks from people who don't read the ad so carefully (cold traffic!). At the same time, if you are on place 5-10, you get much fewer clicks since people go to another site before reading your ad. And if you are not on the first page at all, you typically don't get any traffic at all.

You cannot force Google to place you in the position you want to be. You can only influence the platform's decision by how much you bid (max CPC,) and this changes all the time (since other advertisers are bidding for the same keywords.) It would, hence, take constant updates of your bids if you want to optimize and stay in position 3 (or any other performance metric) for each keyword. But by using the following automated rules, the system will handle this automatically:

RULE NAME	CREATED BY	FREQUENCY	DESCRIPTION
Secure min top 5 position	robert@unitedsurfcamps.com Mar 2. 2014	Daily at 11 AM (GMT+01:00) Stockholm Using data from Same day	Increase bid by kr0.30 Max bid: kr1.70 Requirements: Avg. position worse than 5 Account > All but removed keywords
Secure not top 2 position	robert@unitedsurfcamps.com Mar 2. 2014	Daily at 11 AM (GMT+01:00) Stockholm Using data from Same day	Decrease bid by kr0.35 Min bid: kr0.25 Requirements: Avg. position better than 2 Account > All but removed keywords

The logic behind these rules is:

1. The first rule increases the bid for each keyword that has dropped to a position below 5.
2. The second rule decreases the bid for each keyword that has a better position than 3.

How much to increase/decrease the bids calls for some experimentation. It is also wise to set a cap (maximum bid) you are willing to pay (based on your break-even cost per conversion) and hence, keywords that are too expensive at the moment will automatically not show.

Tip #11: Put on the Autopilot bidding per keyword to save lots of time

Whether you apply the Autopilot based on position or any other metric (e.g., average CPC) depends on your business model, and it needs to be analyzed. Either way, placing your bid choices on autopilot is a great way to daily optimize your campaigns that does not need your constant attention.

Remember what we discussed earlier (in tip # 7) of how to conclude your maximum CPC based on what gross margin you get from each sale.

By applying your maximum CPC in autopilot mode, you don't need to worry so much about exceeding your daily budget.

It is instead better to put a high daily budget, and let the maximum CPC for each keyword set the cap. This way you don't risk losing any potential customers since your ads stop showing once your daily budget is reached.

Tip #12: Release the budget once the business case is proven

Going beyond AdWords

Google has >80% market share among search engines[9]. Therefore, I have so far discussed only opportunities that Google provides.

But once you have ongoing campaigns successfully running on Google, it is time to also consider other search engines. The good news is that the second largest search engine Microsoft's Bing and the third largest search engine Yahoo have joined forces and enable you to advertise on both via one platform: Bing Ads.

Even better news is that Bing/Yahoo have realized that they will never be number one and therefore have applied a very pragmatic strategy to get at least some piece of the cake: automated incorporation of your Google AdWords account into Bing Ads!

Tip #13: Automatically transfer your Google campaign to Bing/Yahoo

Google AdWords and Bing Ads are not corresponding 100%, but still you can sync both systems at least 90% automatically! This means that you can start up a Bing Ads account and have all your Google ads showing on Bing/Yahoo directly (requires approximately one hour of

---

[9] statista.com/statistics/216573/worldwide-market-share-of-search-engines

work.) This will enable you to reach approximately 10% more audience which will vary according to market shares per country and will enable lower bids for the same positions (because of less competition) hence, lower cost per conversion compared to Google.

Even though Google today has over 80% market share, this has not always been the case, and it has varied a lot among different markets. For example, Yahoo has traditionally had a much bigger market share in USA than in Europe. Emerging markets, like Russia and China, have alternative search engines challenging Google domestically[10].

Tip #14: Stay up to date with search market shares and trends while you grow

This means that it makes sense to stay up-to-date with search engine trends and market shares while you grow, i.e., with new markets. It can also be worth it to investigate the position of the local yellow pages' companies in your specific market. As a general rule, the more "local" your business is, the more interesting it can be to use search engine marketing from yellow pages companies.

Summary

In summary, Paid search traffic enables you to target a broad scope of keywords (in a structure that works best for you) and to give direct effect, but it also has many pitfalls to avoid.

To be successful you shall:

---

[10] searchenginejournal.com/differences-between-google-and-its-local-competitors/26006

- ✓ First, focus on Google AdWords, since Google has > 80% market share
- ✓ First, focus only on Search marketing and save Display marketing for later
- ✓ Find your strategic keywords
- ✓ Adapt your campaigns, ads and your website structure based on these keywords
- ✓ Conclude your maximum Cost Per Click, based on your conversion rate and gross margin
- ✓ Put on the autopilot, to save lots of time and automatically optimize your profit
- ✓ Test and improve your ads, using A/B-tests, Ad extensions and Remarketing campaigns
- ✓ Move your campaigns to Bing/Yahoo and local search engines, once AdWords is optimized

In the next chapter, we will discuss how to rank high organically on Google without paying! This practice is obviously more attractive than paying per click, but it requires much more time and fragile work.

The reason this book handles Paid search traffic before Organic search traffic is that the paid one is the fastest one to start testing the business idea. If you can prove the business case when paying for traffic, you have a great potential of future profits and achievement of a top10 organic ranking. But if you cannot prove the business case with paid search traffic, you have most likely entered a niche that is too competitive. In such a case, it will not make sense to spend time and effort to achieve organic ranking.

Practical tips presented in this chapter:

Tip #1: Use "niche" rather than broad keywords

Tip #2: Benchmark competitors' keywords

Tip #3: Use "match types" to avoid cold traffic

Tip #4: Carefully evaluate the best campaign structure

Tip #5: Use A/B test to optimize the ad appearance

Tip #6: Create separate ads and landing pages for each strategic keyword

Tip #7: Track and focus on conversions (not only clicks)

Tip #8: Use ad extensions to facilitate conversions

Tip #9: Focus on real Search traffic - avoid Display network marketing in the start-up

Tip #10: Experiment with Remarketing campaigns

Tip #11: Put on the Autopilot bidding per keyword

Tip #12: Release the budget once the business case is proven

Tip #13: Automatically transfer your Google campaign to Bing/Yahoo

Tip #14: Stay up-to-date with search market shares and trends while you grow

Resources mentioned in chapter 1

✓ **Google Adwords** (adwords.google.com) - The most important tool for Online business.

✓ **Keywordspy** (keywordspy.com) - Tool to "spy" on the keywords that your competitors use.

✓ **Bing Ads** (bingads.microsoft.com) - Platform for ad campaigns using Bing (Microsoft) and Yahoo ads. Key feature is to automatically transfer your ads from Google Adwords.

CHAPTER 2

Maximize (free of charge) organic search traffic

Introduction - What is Search Engine Optimization?

Search engine optimization (SEO) is the art of making your landing pages appear high in the Search Engine Result Page (SERP). To be successful, you must appear on the first page (top 10) for your most valuable keywords.

Unlike Paid search traffic (discussed in chapter 1), Organic search traffic requires long term work and is very sensitive to changes in Google's algorithms.

So, what decides how high your site will rank in Google's organic search result? Google's algorithm is a well-kept secret, and their team constantly updates it, which can have a big impact (positive or negative) on how much organic search traffic your website receives. What we do know is that the algorithm considers over 200 factors in the ranking, but we don't know exactly which they are and how they are valued and interdependent. But in a simplified way, you can say that your position on Google is an equation with three components:

Google organic position = <u>Page authority</u> x <u>Key word relevance</u> x <u>Site Performance</u>

These three components and the best practices to optimize them are discussed in detail in the remaining part of this chapter. However, there is one more "ingredient" in this equation: <u>clickability</u>. Once you appear in the Top10 organic search, you have completed 75% of your work. The rest is about making results "clickable" by users (discussed in Tip #30 and #31.)

Page Authority - How to get quality links to your website

One of the reasons that Google has been so successful in matching search queries with the most relevant content is that they, from the early days, have traced and ranked how websites are linking to each other.

<u>Page Rank</u> is a metric named after Google's founder Larry Page which measures the "general importance" of a website. It is mainly based

on how many other websites are linking to your website. It also looks at the importance of the page that contains the link.

Pages with higher Page Rank have more weight in "voting" with their links than pages with lower Page Rank. It also looks at the number of outgoing links on the page "giving the vote." The value from the votes is then shared equally by all outgoing links. This makes sense, because people tend to link to relevant content. Therefore, websites with more links to them are usually better.

Page Rank is measured on a scale of 0-10. New websites start with page rank 0 and then the more that other websites start linking to it, the higher the page rank rises. However, this is a logarithmic scale meaning that it is much harder to go from rank 6 to 7, compared to going from rank 2 to 3. You can check what Page Rank your and your competitors' websites have by using one of many free tools available online (e.g. checkpagerank.net/.)

Page Rank was an extremely important factor in the early days of search engine optimization, but during the last years it has faded in importance. This is due to the fact that page rank was fairly easy to manipulate by building up the number of sites linking to each other (so called link farms.) Over the years Google has made continuous updates in the search algorithm to include other factors affecting the ranking.

Google still publishes the Page Rank for all websites, but it is only updated around twice per year. This paved the ground for another more advanced ranking factor, called Page Authority, which is provided by Moz.com.

Moz scores the page authority of each website on a 100-point, logarithmic scale. Meaning that it is easier to grow your score from 10 to 20 than it is to grow from 70 to 80. Besides ranking each website, it also gives a score of the top domain, called <u>Domain Authority</u>.

Unlike Page Rank, the Page Authority provided by Moz is regularly updated, and it includes additional factors that give a better indication of the "general importance" of your website for Google. The Page Authority algorithm is recalibrated every time Google makes updates in its search algorithm, with the aim to provide the best possible indication of how well a given webpage is likely to rank in Google's search results at any point of time.

The Page Authority and domain authority of any given website can be checked at http://moz.com/researchtools/ose/. You can also install it as a tool bar directly in your web browser: http://moz.com/tools/seo-toolbar.

So how can you increase your Page Authority? Since Google is constantly changing its algorithm, the Page Authority algorithm is also constantly updated. However, in a simplified form there are five main categories to consider:

1. <u>Quantity and quality of incoming links</u> - Basically the same as Page Rank.
2. <u>Diversity of incoming links</u> - It is better to have a few links from many different sites than it is to have a large number of incoming links from a few sites. Hence, the number of linking domains is more important than the absolute number of links.
3. <u>Quantity and quality of outgoing links</u> - Concerns how trustworthy you are in using your link voting. Linking to authority sites has a positive effect, while linking to spam domains can be devastating.
4. <u>Trustworthiness of your domain</u> - Older domains are considered more trustworthy than new ones. The type of incoming links to your domain is also important. For example, links from

universities and government are considered more trustworthy, while links from spam sites have a negative impact. Another factor is the trustworthiness of other domains registered in your name.

5. <u>Traffic measures</u> - Including number of returning visitors, number of page views per visitor, time spent on the page and the user bounce rate and how consistent the traffic is over time.

The most important factor is to have trustworthy websites linking to you. Note that quality is more important than quantity when it comes to links. If you could get one website with a high Page Authority (e.g., 70) to link to your site while not linking to many other sites, this would be worth much more than hundreds of links from sites with low Page Authority and many outgoing links.

So how to get quality links? First of all, there are many websites with high Page Authority where you can be in control of putting a link to your website. Most obvious ones are company pages on Facebook, Twitter, LinkedIn, YouTube, etc. (further discussed in tip #32, #33 and #34.)

There are also many niche platforms with similar logic. For example, unitedsurfcamps.com has supported kiva.org for long time. (Kiva is a micro-loans platform for small entrepreneurs in developing countries.) A positive side effect of this is that we have an ingoing link to our team site from there. (Feel invited to support a good cause at: <u>kiva.org/team/surf travelers</u>.)

Another thing to consider is if you might have additional websites within your network? For instance, maybe you or some of your friends have blogs or their own websites where you can place a link? Or maybe it is worthwhile to create a separate website which will be easier to get PR links to? You can then transfer most of the Page

Authority from this website to your main website (by only having outgoing links to this).

Tip #15: Post your URL on websites you have direct access to

Thousands of "Open directories" websites exist where you can insert a link to your website manually. Although it is an easy way to get many links, these links tend to have very low value since there are so many outgoing links sharing the "voting." You also need to consider there is fine line between an "open directory" and a "link farm." We don't know which websites have been blacklisted by Google but for sure you will come across a few if you use this technique widely. Hence this technique shall either be avoided or only used on websites you are sure to be trustworthy.

Another medium where you can manually insert links is in the comment fields on blogs and forums. This has so far not been considered by Google as something which shall be punished. However, you will most likely be banned by the blog or forum moderators and get a negative impact of your brand if you just push your website without adding any relevant content to the discussion.

The above techniques are all examples of where you can be in control of manually creating links to your website The next level of link generation is to take an active approach in exchanging links with other websites. You start by creating a long list of websites which have both high value (high page rank but low outgoing links) and high probability to get a link from. One of the best tips to evaluate the "probability" is to check who is linking to your competitors. For example, try the help of moz.com/researchtools/ose.

You then contact the website asking to exchange links. If you have had a website up and running for some time, I am sure you have received an e-mail at some point from a webmaster of another site asking to trade links?

Tip #16: Actively manage a Link exchange program

Just note there is a fine balance to "manipulate" your incoming links. During recent years Google has created many refinements in their algorithm which affect how high they rank different websites.

One example is that Google now rates how related the content is on the website that links to you is to your content. This means that it is OK to conduct some link exchanges and get links from forums and directories, if the sites where the links come from are trustworthy and have relevant content for your website. This means that when unitedsurcamps.com receives links from surf shops or surf forum it is relevant. But if unitedsurfcamps.com for example receives many incoming links from websites selling jewelry, open directories without a theme, or forums discussing child care, such is a "yellow flag" for Google.

Another update in Google's algorithm is that they today look for and punish websites with "unnatural link patterns." I had a tough experience with unitedsurfcamps.com regarding this. Just over a few days our organic search traffic from Google dropped 30% (see graph below).

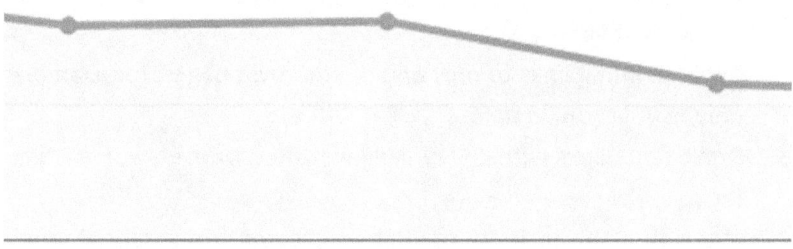

April 2013   May 2013   June 2013

In a normal season the traffic to unitedsurfcamps.com is higher in June than in May, but in June 2013 the organic search traffic instead dropped 30% and continued to stay on the lower level. After some investigation I tracked-back the drop to a major Google algorithm update on 23rd of May 2013, called Penguin 2.0. This update downgraded some of the links we got and instead favored competition. Hence, a few of our most strategic keywords dropped below Top10 which had a 30% impact on total organic traffic.

Before the Google update, I had worked actively with tip #15 and tip #16 above. To optimize the values of each link I had used anchor texts (the "clickable" text in the link) which corresponded to our strategic key words (further described in tip #2.1) For example, almost all links to our top domain had the anchor text "surf camp" while a link to the landing page for Surf Camp Algarve, had the anchor text "Surf camp Algarve."

The update in Google's algorithm started to look for what they call "unnatural link patterns", to be able to discover websites that had manipulated (too much) to gain their incoming links.

Tip #17: Make sure you have a natural link pattern

The key success factors to ensure you have a natural link pattern are:

1. Don't use the same anchor text repeatedly - Google looks for anchor text variety
2. Avoid pointing links to only one of your own pages, for example, only to your top domain
3. Don't trade links with low ranking websites, or even worse - "link farms"
4. Make sure the majority of your links come from websites with content that relates to yours

5. Build links slowly over time - as this looks more natural
6. Surround the links with text (e.g., "check out this <u>surf camp</u> for more info")

Concerning the first point (to have varied anchor texts) you shall strive to have an even distribution (10-20% share) of the seven anchor text categories below:

1. <u>Exact match</u> -The anchor text is exactly the same as your strategic key word (e.g., "surf camp")
2. <u>Phrase match</u> - The anchor text includes your keyword plus other words (e.g., "book surf camp")
3. <u>Brand Name</u> - The anchor text is your brand or domain name (e.g., unitedsurfcamps.com
4. <u>Keyword Branded</u> - The anchor text combines your brand name and keywords such as "book surf camp at unitedsurfcamps.com
5. <u>Branded</u> - The anchor text includes your brand name, plus some other words, but not your keywords, for example, "travel with unitedsurfcamps.com"
6. <u>Other</u> - The anchor text includes some random text and/or some other keywords, but not your main keyword (e.g.," book a surf trip)"
7. <u>URL</u> - The anchor text is just your website URL (e.g., <u>www.unitedsurfcamps.com</u>)

In the case of unitedsurfcamps.com, I had over 50% of or links as exact match (category 1) when Google released the Penguin 2.0 update in May 2013, and hence, we got hit hard! Since then we have worked to step by step build up a natural link pattern and climb back in the rankings, but it takes lot of time and effort which could have been avoided if we hadn't "over-optimized" our link building from the start.

Today the SEO community discusses "white hat" vs. "black hat" techniques, where black hat refers to overdoing link exchange, building up link farms, overstuffing links and websites with keywords. The common view is that the days of "black hat" are over and instead website owners need to focus on "white hat" techniques, meaning building fresh quality content and working with PR.

The core concept of "white hat" is to get your website mentioned in articles, blogs and in other online media. This can happen by itself. For example, one of the most valuable links for unitedsurfcamps.com comes from bbc.com which wrote an article about surfing and linked to unitedsurfcamp.com as an example. However this is not something you can count on and is most probable for companies with recognizable brands or dominant market share.

The most effective technique is hence to work proactively with PR, either on your own or by engaging a PR-agency. This is often referred to as content marketing and is based on three main tactics you (or your agency) can apply:

1. Create your own articles and blogs related to your business - When the content you write can answer questions that people are looking for you will sure get natural links from other blogs and websites.

2. Engage bloggers to write about you - Or offer to write a guest blog at their website (with a link to you) which must be a "win-win." Possibly cover the same topics as suggested in the first point, but the content is published on an external site and the link to your website is in the text.

3. Position yourself as an expert in your niche - One great free resource is HARO, Help a reporter out, where you can register as a subject matter expert and be automatically contacted when a reporter is looking for expertise you possess. You can also go one

step further and use a PR-agency to write articles about, you which are then offered to a magazine as a freelance article.

Here is a Top10 example of topics for articles and blogs. After each topic I have given an example from unitedsurfcamps.com:

1. In-depth advice connected with your offering - Additional travel tips when visiting Morocco
2. "How-to" guides - How surfer can train their skills even when there are no waves
3. Interviews with a celebrity in your niche - Interviews with the surf coach of the national team
4. Test pilot - Surfing on an artificial wave in the desert of Dubai
5. Common "mistakes to be avoided" - Why many surfers fail to develop their surfing skills
6. News summary - Surf news highlights of 2015
7. Historic event - How the first surfboard was invented
8. Statistics - How many shark attacks on surfers occur each year
9. Case studies - How a student association learned how to surf and party during spring break
10. Clarifications - Glossary of terms being used in surfing and what they actually mean

Note that all of the above topics can be explored fairly easy by yourself, if you just make some background check and start building a network in your niche. Neither do they require that you visit different industry events nor that you will be the first one to report on the subject.

Just be sure that you write unique content and just don't "copy-paste" texts from other websites, as this kind of duplicate content is downgraded by Google.

Tip #18: Work proactively with PR, to get the most valuable links

Besides producing "text content" in articles and blogs, you can also create more advanced content that will be engaging for people to interact with. For example:

1. Launch a competition
2. Create a free tool, game or plug-in for download
3. Make a quiz or voting poll
4. Create a smart Infographics
5. Make a Funny video

All the above can be perceived as valuable to many people and could trigger natural links and social media mentions (which are further discussed in next chapter.)

There are many free tools available where you can track how your brand name and website are being mentioned (with and without proper links) on websites and in social media. Test some tools such as Google Alerts or Mention.com.

Just remember to have an "online" perspective on your PR activities. It is not enough that your company is being mentioned in the article or blog; your target is to get a link (with suitable anchor text!) to your website.

If you are mentioned in an article without a link, it still has some value of brand recognition for the people reading the article. It is also some help for your SEO since Google will associate your brand name with relevant content and trustworthiness; however, it would be much more beneficial for you if there also is a link to your website. If there is no link, it can be worth it to contact the article author and ask if they will include a link to your website. Accomplish this to increase the value and make more sense for the article readers.

Besides receiving links to your website, it has during recent years also become important to get "social endorsements" to rank high on search engines.

This is an example of how social endorsements buttons have been incorporated at unitedsurfcamps.com:

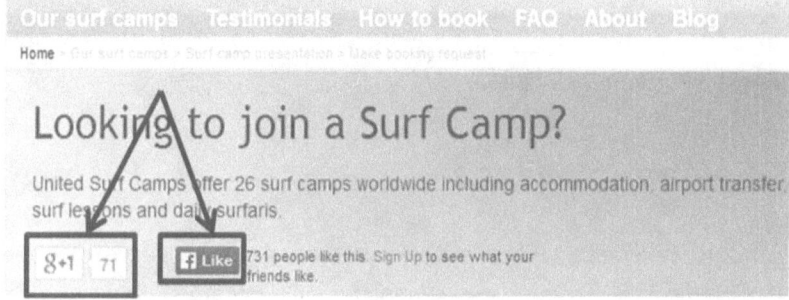

Besides increasing the Page Authority of the site, these endorsements have a direct rank boosting effect on users searching for keywords connected to what somebody in their social networks has endorsed.

This means that somebody searching for "surf camp" will see unitedsurfcamps.com on position 1 (instead of, for example, position 5) if he is logged into his Google account and has a friend who has previously clicked the g+1 button at unitedsurfcamps.com.

Tip #19: Use social endorsement buttons

In a similar way, your ranking for a specific user can also be influenced by "local factors." If you have listed the address of your store locations properly on Google My Business, you will rank higher for somebody in close geographic distance to your physical location.

Tip #20: Use local search ranking factors (listing correct store locations, etc.)

It can also affect the appearance and hence the "clickability" (discussed in Tip #30 and #31) of your search result by showing a Google map with your location directly in the search result.

In summary, having many qualitative incoming links and social endorsements will improve your general ranking. But even if your competitors have higher general page authority, you can still outrank them for specific keywords, if you have better keyword relevance on that specific landing page.

Keyword relevance

Keyword relevance refers to how common a certain keyword is on your dedicated landing page. When the keyword a user is searching for occurs in logically important places on the landing page, this tells Google that the website is relevant for this keyword and, as a result, will rank it higher.

For example:

1. You search for "sports shoes" in Google
2. There is company X and company Y in the search results
3. Company X used the phrase "sports shoes" 5 times on their landing page
4. Company Y used it 3 times
5. Which company has higher "Keyword Relevance?"

The obvious answer is company X (5 times vs. Y: 3 times). But what if Company Y used the search term in more "logically important" places, like in the headline or in the domain name? This would actually enable higher key word relevance than company X (assuming that the keyword only occurred in the normal text here.)

Not that a "keyword" can consist of many different words. It can even be a whole sentence like: "The best running shoes for winter." Actually "key phrase" is a better term to describe this, but "keyword" is what is most commonly used in the SEO industry.

Keywords can be divided in three main groups, based on how specific they are:

1. Obsolete keywords - Keywords that are too general to optimize a landing page. The competition is too high and even if you would rank high, it would not generate much "hot traffic" since there are so many different needs behind the phrase. Example of these kind of keywords are "surf," "surfing," and "Surf Morocco."

2. Main keywords - Keywords that are specific enough to drive "hot traffic", but still general enough to drive high search volumes. For example: "surf camp," "surf camp morocco," "surf school," "surf school morocco."

3. Long tail keywords - Keywords which are very specific and hence have less competition in the ranking, but also lower search volumes. For example "best surf school for women in morocco."

Each landing page shall be targeted for one main keyword such as "surf camp Morocco." If you try to get the landing page optimized for more keywords, i.e., "accommodation Morocco" and "travel Morocco," Google will be confused and you will rather end up with low rankings (not Top10) for too many keywords.

Besides your main keyword, it is beneficial to also optimize each landing page for 3-7 additional long tail keywords, which are naturally clustered with the main key word. For example, when doing research for the launch of this book, I concluded to start building five landing pages with the following set-up:

Main keyword:		Landing page 1 start online business	Landing page 2 profitable online business	Landing page 3 Internet home business	Landing page 4 start e-commerce	Landing page 5 start e-business
Long tail keywords:	1	online business startup	most profitable online business	home based internet business	e-commerce startup	e-business startup
	2	set up online business	profitable online business ideas	home based online business	set up e-commerce	set up e-business
	3	new online business	successful online business	internet online business	new e-commerce	new e-business
	4	to do online business	make money online business	work at home online business	to do e-commerce	to do e-business
	5	online business tips	best online business	online business work from home	e-commerce tips	e-business tips

Here is a Top10 guide to optimize the keyword relevance of each landing page:

1. The domain name of each landing page shall be short, readable and include the main keyword. Example: unitedsurfcamps.com/surf-camp/Morocco target "surf camp Morocco"
2. Unique title text including the main keyword for each landing page
3. Unique meta description for each landing page (does not need to include the keyword)
4. Unique main headline <h1> including the main keyword for each landing page
5. Sub headlines <h2> including the main keyword or long tail keywords
6. Internal links shall be text (not pictures) and include the main keyword or long tail keywords
7. The keywords occur in <alt-tags> on pictures
8. The keywords occur in file name of pictures
9. The keywords occur many times in the text, but not too frequently so it is considered as "spammy" by Google

10. Use also synonyms and variations of the keyword order such as "morocco surf camps" instead of "surf camp morocco" to not look "over-optimized" from Google's perspective

Tip #21: Optimize keyword position density per landing page

Just note that there is a fine trade-off between creating a website with high keyword relevance vs. creating a "keyword spammed" site. If Google determines your site to be of the second type, it will have a very bad influence on your rankings, so be careful, test and iterate.

Another important factor is that Google discredits duplicate content. This means that if you have many landing pages with the same page titles, text, meta descriptions and such, but you only change selected keywords, Google will be suspicious and consider it as "spammy."

Tip #22: Avoid duplicate content

It is therefore of great importance that you have as much unique text and pictures on each landing page as possible. Of course, there may be a trade-off between usability and site structure. But it can still be worth it to not use the same generic content on several pages unless they are adding value to the sales funnel (discussed in Chapter 4.).

This also means that you need to choose the most strategic keywords in your organic search effort since it will be very hard to build and manage hundreds of landing pages with totally unique content.

This is the same logic as we discussed in chapter 1 (Paid traffic) tip #6 - to create separate ads and landing pages for each strategic keyword. In chapter 1, we motivated it by achieving a high "quality score" and hence, minimized the cost per click. In this chapter (Organic traffic) we motivate it by choosing the keywords we can get the most "free of charge" traffic for and therefore is worth the effort to create unique content for.

As an example, the landing page structure on unitedsurfcamps.com is based on the structure:

"surf camp <camp-name>", for example, "Surf camp Morocco" or "Surf camp Mexico".

There is no unique landing page which has "surf holiday Morocco" or "learn to surf Morocco" as the main keyword, since it would be too much effort to create a unique structure (without duplicate data) for these secondary keywords.

This is based on the conclusion that "surf camp" is a more strategic keyword than "surf holiday" and "learn to surf," based on market size and competition (as discussed in the introduction chapter.)

Keyword (by relevance)	Avg. monthly searches ? Jun 2014	Competition ?
surf camp morocco	480	Medium
surf school morocco	170	Low
surf holiday morocco	70	Medium
learn to surf morocco	40	Low

The term "surf school morocco" (along with the same logic for the remaining 24 surf camps) looks more interesting. Maybe it would be worth the effort to build unique landing pages for it? On the other hand, it can still be targeted as a long tail keyword for the landing page for "surf camp Morocco" and via paid search traffic.

One common pitfall regarding duplicate content is that your website can be accessed both with and without the www- prefix. The funny thing is that Google and other search engines then consider this as two different websites with the exact duplicate content! Therefore you shall decide which one is the master (unitedsurfcamps.com or www.unitedsurfcamps.com) and use a "301 redirect link" from the secondary option.

Another way to handle this and other duplication errors that could occur (especially if your site has a search function for several dimensions) is to use what Google calls "canonical" tagging. This means that even if the same content could appear on several pages, you clearly markup which one is the "master page" that the specific content belongs to.

Tip #23: Use redirect or canonical links to make sure the right pages are indexed

The duplication pitfall together with high keyword competition have a big impact on how you set up your landing page structure. It is important that you avoid "keyword cannibalization," meaning that you have more than one landing page that targets the same keyword. This confuses Google about which landing page is more important for the specific keyword and affects your rankings negatively.

It is also important to consider how deep hierarchy you build the landing page structure on. Google will give you lower and lower ranking the further down in hierarchy from the top domain that the landing page occurs.

For example, consider the following structure (keywords in bold):

✓ Level 1: **Surf Camp** (unitedsurfcamps.com)
✓ Level 2: Our 25 **Surf camps** (unitedsurfcamps.com/our-surf-camps)
✓ Level 3: **Surf camps** in **Europe** (unitedsurfcamps.com/our-surf-camps/europe)

- ✓ Level 4: **Surf Camps** in **Portugal** (unitedsurfcamps.com/ our-surf-camps/europe/ Portugal)
- ✓ Level 5: **Surf Camp Lisbon** (unitedsurfcamps.com/our-surf-camps/europe/ Portugal/Lisbon)
- ✓ Level 5: **Surf Camp Porto** (unitedsurfcamps.com/our-surf-camps/europe/ Portugal/Porto)

This structure enables you to target several levels of broadness in keywords (surf camp; Surf camps; Surf camps Europe; Surf camps Portugal; Surf camp Lisbon), but the problem is that the most important landing pages "surf camp Lisbon" and "surf camp Porto," in this case, come on hierarchy level 5, which is very bad for their ranking.

Hence a better structure we discovered for unitedsurfcamps.com is the following:

- ✓ Level 1:**Surf Camp** (unitedsurfcamps.com)
- ✓ Level 2: Our 25 **Surf camps** (unitedsurfcamps.com/our-surf-camps)
- ✓ Level 3: **Surf Camp Lisbon** (unitedsurfcamps.com/surf-camp/Lisbon)
- ✓ Level 3: **Surf Camp Porto** (unitedsurfcamps.com/surf-camp/Porto)

In this case, the most important landing pages are already on hierarchy level 3 and hence get better ranking. The downside of this structure is that it is missing pages that optimize for the keywords "Surf camps Europe" and "Surf camps Portugal" which hence need to instead be targeted on separate landing pages without duplicating content or covering up with paid search traffic (discussed in chapter 1.)

A good idea is to investigate your competitors and see what keywords they are targeting in what type of hierarchy. If you see competitors go too deep in their hierarchy, such could be an opportunity for you.

You can also affect part of the hierarchy with the way you use internal links, for example, the top domain link pointed directly to a very important product on hierarchy level 3.

The key idea is to base your landing page structure on keywords, meaning what people actually search for (discussed in chapter 1.) It is tempting to just input the category names and product names that you have in your product portfolio, but if they are not the same keywords (or hierarchy) as people actually search for on Google, the keyword phrasing must be adapted.

Tip #24: Choose landing page structure based on keyword relevance (not internal factors)

But what about keywords that your analysis shows is less important? Besides targeting them with Paid Search traffic (chapter 1), you can also create dedicated pages such as via your blog. With a blog, you can for example optimize each post for a keyword that you aren't targeting with the main landing pages on your site.

Tip #25: Use your blog to target additional "long tail" keywords

Just note that there is no success to be found in writing blogs stuffed to the extreme with your targeted keyword. When writing for your blog, focus on developing great content on topics that people will want to read and share; this will drive the ranking up. If the blog post appears to "spammy," Google could downgrade not only the blog post but your whole domain.

Also consider that there are three different "objectives" to choose from when writing a blog post:

1. To get natural links (discussed in tip #17 and tip #18 above)
2. To capture potential customers searching for "niche keywords (tip #25 above)"
3. To use the blog post as endorsements to motivate customers to make a conversion (further discussed in tip# 50 in chapter 4)

Besides your landing pages (which are always a target for one main keyword and 3-7 long tail keywords), you would typically have several other pages in your site hierarchy which you do not want to optimize. This can, for example, be in lower hierarchy pages such as in the "about us"-section such as company history or your payment process. These pages need to exist from a usability point of view but not from a search engine point of view. The risk is that they include some of the keywords from your landing pages (cannibalization) and hence affect the ranking of these landing pages negatively (especially if they are on a lower hierarchy level.)

Tip #26: Actively manage what sites NOT to be indexed as well

The best way to handle this is to minimize internal links to "non-landing pages" and place the following meta tag into the <head> section of the page NOT to be indexed:

<meta name="robots" content="noindex">

Things to remember:

✓ Understand what is the size of potential traffic for each keyword
✓ Understand how strong the competition is for each keyword

✓ Conclude a site structure based on landing pages which each target 1 strategic keyword and 3-7 long tail keywords

✓ Build and optimize keyword dense landing pages in this structure, avoiding duplicate content

✓ Consider using blog posts to target additional keywords, which are not covered on any landing page

✓ Keep in mind that there will always be a trade-off between user-friendliness and the keyword-driven website structure

Site performance

The third main factor affecting how well you rank on Google and other search engines is the site performance. This means how easy and safe it is to access and use your website.

The first hygienic factor is to make sure that there are no errors in the website and that you follow the very latest HTML standards.

Tip #27: Follow latest HTML standards

This can be easily checked by logging into Google Webmaster Tools. This is a free of charge tool that can give you many insights in how your website is being perceived by Google and if there are any issues to be addressed. If you have any issues you will get excellent guidance in how to restore them by following the instructions on Google support pages.

In the last few years, the graphic design and functionality of websites have become more advanced and sophisticated, which increases loading times. In order to address this issue, Google has started to discredit sites that have long loading times.

Tip #28: Monitor and improve the page speed

As a rule of thumb, page speed would be an issue if it takes more than 3 seconds for your website to load. There are many available free tools that help you measure and diagnose the potential issues with your site loading times (e.g., tools.pingdom.com.)

In that case you should try to diagnose the root cause, which can be either of two main sources:

1. External - If the problem is with your web hotel's capacity, you can either buy more server space or change web hotel.
2. Internal - The issue may be your website code. You can recode the HTML and CMS or reduce image and file sizes.

Another important factor is website safety (i.e., not easy to hack.) You can confirm this via several free online tools (e.g. detectify.com.)

Tip #29: Enable high security level

In July 2014, Google announced that they will place higher and higher weight on security in the organic ranking factor[11]. Specifically they mentioned that implementation of basic encryption of the data using HTTPS (instead of HTTP) will affect ranking more and more.

Another factor with your site performance is that it is working well on different platforms, including smartphones and tablets with various screen sizes. This can have a big effect on your conversion rate for these devices and is discussed in detail in tip #60 of chapter 4. However, the responsiveness of your website on different devices has also been included as a ranking factor by Google, meaning that if

---

[11] googleonlinesecurity.blogspot.co.uk/2014/08/https-as-ranking-signal_6.html

your website is not suitable for tablets and smartphones, it will affect your ranking in a negative way.

Google offers concrete tips about what should be changed to improve both the page speed and user-friendliness in mobile devices. Check out: https://developers.google.com/speed/pagespeed/insights.

Click ability

So, you have been successful with optimizing the equation:

Page Rank x Keyword Relevance x Site Performance.

Chances are high that you have outperformed enough competitors to appear on Google's first page (Top10). Congratulations!

However, it is not enough to be visible on Top10 organic search list; potential customers must also choose to click on your listing (and not a competitor's) to actually come to your site and make a conversion. Hence, the fourth important factor to consider is "clickability".

What makes you click on a search result? Using common sense, it shall be a clear title and description to confirm that the site contains what you are looking for.

However, there may be a trade-off between making a website "clickable" and optimizing it to rank high on Google. So, if you are "too strategic" when inserting your keywords (e.g., the title and meta description of the landing pages) this will make much more sense for the search engine, than for a human who prefer that which does not feel contrived.

Tip #30: Find best trade-off between writing headline and intro for Robots vs. Real users

The good news is that Google also takes click through rate (CTR) into considerations in the rankings. This means that if you get many people to click on your listing, it will over time appear higher in the search result.

A best practice is to include a "unique selling point" (USP) in the meta description. Here are a few examples:

- ✓ Travel insurance - Get a price quote in 30 seconds!
- ✓ Design cufflinks - Free delivery worldwide!
- ✓ Ergonomic pillows - 100% money back guarantee the first year!

Google also considers the "dwell time," meaning how long time an average visitor spends on your site before going back to the search result. It is hence very important that you keep "the promise" you make in the search result.

One factor that has been sort of a revolution for "clickability" is rich snippets.

Study the search results below:

Carve Surf Morocco | Surf Camp taking you to Morocco's ...
www.carvesurfmorocco.com/ ▼
Surf camp holidays taking you to the premier surf breaks in Morocco, and surf school
packages for the ultimate surf adventure. Whether you want to learn to surf, ...

Surf Camp Morocco
www.unitedsurfcamps.com › Our surf camps ▼
★★★★✦ Rating: 4.3 - 105 votes - €340.00
Surf camp Morocco is located in the calm surf village of Tamraght, 15 km north of
Agadir and 4 km south of Taghazoute, at the Atlantic coast of Morocco.

He'e nalu **surf camp Morocco**
www.heenalusurfcamp.com/ ▼
Discover our **Surf camp** in **Morocco** " South of Agadir " ... Looking for Surf Guiding in
Morocco, but would like to surf away from the crowed and ride the best spots ...

Surf Morocco, Surf Taghazout, **Surf** holiday Morocco, **Surfi**...
www.**surf**taghazout.com/ ▼
Surfing Morocco, Surf Taghazout offers surf holiday in Morocco, beach front surf ...
Taghazout surf camp packages with **surf lessons** and surf coaching fit for ...

Which one would you click on? The one with the pretty yellow stars, right?

"Rich snippets" was introduced by Google to help the search engine better understand the components of your website. The technique can be applied to many different cases (events, recipes, people, etc.) but where I find it most useful for e-commerce is in tagging product reviews and product prices (as shown in the example above.)

Tip #31: Use "rich snippets" to show your products directly in the search result

The content on your website can be easily tagged with rich snippets via Google Webmaster tools.

Summary

In summary, ranking high organically with your most strategic keywords can have an awesome impact on your business. But you need to be aware that it is also a very uncertain situation since Google is constantly updating their algorithm.

Ranking high organically require you to optimize the function
Page Authority x Keyword Relevance x Site Performance

The most challenging part in this equation is the Page Authority. Be prepared that it usually requires long term dedicated work (or big investments in a PR-agency) to get enough quality links from quality sites to reach a high Page Authority. But once you are successful, it is a great base for getting free traffic for many different keywords.

The Keyword Relevance is very connected to the work you do to optimize Paid Search traffic (discussed in chapter 1.) For your most strategic keywords, build keyword-dense landing pages so you will rank higher organically than your competitors. You can also add 3-7 Long tail keywords as secondary keywords on each landing page or target them with blog posts or just by Paid traffic.

The Site Performance has become more and more important in Google's algorithm over the years. To optimize the site performance, you need to make sure there are no errors in your html-code. Be sure to minimize the loading time, using https-protection and ensure responsiveness for different devices.
Finally, remember about "clickability". Use rich snippets and unique selling points in the meta description to look more attractive on the search engine result page.

Practical tips presented in this chapter:

Tip #15: Post your URL on websites you have direct access to

Tip #16: Actively manage a Link exchange program

Tip #17: Make sure you have a natural link pattern

Tip #18: Work proactively with PR, to get the most valuable links

Tip #19: Use social endorsement buttons

Tip #20: Use local search ranking factors (listing correct store locations, etc.)

Tip #21: Optimize keyword position density per landing page

Tip #22: Avoid duplicate content

Tip #23: Use redirect or canonical links to make sure the right pages are indexed

Tip #24: Choose landing page structure based on keyword relevance (not internal factors)

Tip #25: Use your blog to target additional "long tail" keywords

Tip #26: Actively manage what sites NOT to be indexed as well

Tip #27: Follow latest HTML standards

Tip #28: Monitor and improve the page speed

Tip #29: Enable high security level

Tip #30: Find best trade-off between writing headline and intro for Robots vs. Real users

Tip #31: Use "rich snippets" to show your products directly in the search result

Resources mentioned in chapter 2

Competition Benchmarking:

✓ **Check Page Rank** (checkpagerank.net) - Service to check your competitors' page rank
✓ **MOZ Research Tools** (moz.com/researchtools/ose) - Service to check yours and others Page Authority. You can also see who is linking to your competitors (and hence could be willing to link also to you).

Analyze Your Webpage:

✓ **Google Webmaster Tools** (google.com/webmasters) - Free tool that gives you many insights in how your website is being perceived by Google. Here you can also tag the content with rich snippets.
✓ **Google My Business** (google.com/business) - Free tool that enables you to adapt how your business is being perceived in Google Maps by including your phone number and other factors to make you rank better in local search.
✓ **Google Developers** (developers.google.com/speed/pagespeed/insights) - Free tool where you get an evaluation of how user-friendly and fast your website is to use on computers and mobile devices, including concrete tips to resolve detected issues.
✓ **Pingdom** (tools.pingdom.com) - Free tool to check your website loading page and diagnose potential reasons for long loading times.

✓ **Detectify** (detectify.com) - Service that checks the level of security of your webpage.

PR tools:

✓ **HARO (Help a Reporter Out)** (helpareporter.com) - Platform that connects journalists and experts. By "helping a reporter out" you may earn valuable links and establish new relationships.

✓ **Google Alerts** (google.com/alerts) - Tool that notifies you (e.g., via e-mail) every time a chosen keyword (e.g. your company name) is found in a new place on the Internet.

✓ **Mention** (mention.com) - Similar tool like Google Alerts, but with more functionalities.

CHAPTER 3

Synergize with other (non-search) traffic sources

Introduction - The dual benefits of referral traffic

In the first two chapters we discussed the key success factors to get traffic from search engines, both paid and organic. In this chapter we will explore how to acquire traffic from sources other than search engines. This traffic is often called "referral traffic" and has dual benefits:

1. Generate direct "hot traffic" which may convert at your landing page.
2. Generate links that boost your page rank in organic search (as discussed in Tip #16 and #21.)

Referral traffic can also help to build your status as a trustworthy company, but only if you keep the "off-site" data up to date (further discussed in chapter 4).

There are three main types of "non-search traffic sources": <u>Social Media traffic</u>, <u>Online Ads</u> and <u>"Offline" marketing.</u>

Social Media traffic

"Social media" has been the biggest "buzz word" in online marketing in the last decade. There have been many "social start-ups," and the field constantly evolves in exciting ways. But in practice, it has boiled down to having Facebook as the core ingredient of the "soup."

Besides Facebook, other social media channels include:

✓ Direct substitutes such as Twitter, Instagram and Google+.
✓ Social networks with a specific niche (e.g., LinkedIn, Foursquare)
✓ Content sites that have later added on social media platforms (e.g., YouTube and Spotify)
✓ More traditional forms of Social Media (used before Facebook) such as newsletters, blogs and discussion forums

But if you should start somewhere, it is with Facebook (using the same logic that you should start your SEO with Google and not Bing/Yahoo) and then once you have it working, spread your influence to other channels.

The first step is to create a company page on Facebook where you can post engaging content and interact with potential customers.

But how do you reach thousands of "likes" on your Facebook page? The smart thing is that every time somebody makes an active click to "like" your page, it is seen in the news stream of this person, visible for all people in his network. This creates a "viral" effect, meaning that it spreads from one "population" to another.

However to get this viral effect started, either create some awesome engaging content that "goes viral" by itself (by people sharing and referring to this awesome content on your page) or you can acquire likes "inorganically" by paying for them.

Tip #32: Use Facebook ads to build a critical mass of likes on your Facebook page

By using Facebook ads in the startup phase, you can quickly achieve a critical mass of people liking your page and continue driving your "social reach" organically.

Facebook ads show your page as a "recommendation" to Facebook users within your chosen target group (e.g., age, gender, nationality, interest.) Then after acquiring the first set of fans, the "killer" function is that you can choose to spread this only to people connected with people who already "liked" your page. In this case, it will say, for example, "Mark Smith likes this" as a social endorsement under the ad, enabling a much higher conversion rate of Mark's friends.

So let's say you have acquired a few thousand fans which are people have clicked "like" on your Facebook page. What will you use this for? The obvious usage is to drive people to your landing pages where they can make conversions (further discussed in chapter 4) and generate income for you. This is most effectively done by posting engaging content and special promotions, stimulating your Facebook "fans" to visit your website (e.g., "10% discount on product X for all our Facebook fans, until midnight.")

Based on the outcome of these campaigns, you can conclude if it is worth using Facebook ads to get more likes. If it is not, due to low conversion rates, you can stop the ads and just continue to get links organically. By posting interesting content that is "liked" by your "followers," it will be seen by their friends and hence, you will continue to steadily grow your likes without needing ads.

So far we have basically discussed how to use Facebook as a "marketing channel." However, Facebook also has another great benefit: it can be used as a customer service channel.

Tip #33: Use Facebook both as a marketing channel and customer service channel

By allowing your "followers" to post questions on your Facebook page, you can use it as an interaction channel with the clients. This is often a lower "barrier" for the potential customer to make contact than sending you an e-mail. The answer to the questions can be seen by other people visiting your Facebook page which is not the case if they send an e-mail.

Having a critical mass of Facebook fans (at least a few thousand) and using Facebook as an open customer service channel helps build trust among others (further discussed in Tip #45). As a result, the probability increases that more people will consider buying a product or service from you.

When you have your Facebook page under control and have gained some experience in harvesting the benefits, it is time to consider other social networks.

If you have plenty of resources, there is almost no end to how much time and money you can invest in social media experiments. But for most online entrepreneurs, I recommend a more passive strategy where you synergize additional social networks in relation to your current Facebook statuses, activities and updates.

Tip #34: Synergize Facebook with other social media channels

Technically, you integrate your Facebook stream with your Twitter account, your Twitter account with your LinkedIn account, etc. When you send a newsletter or write a blog post, you post a link on your Facebook page (which is then automatically transformed to e.g., Twitter and Instagram.)

In general, the user's acceptance of high frequency of "social buzz" (updates) seems to be higher on e.g., Twitter, Instagram and Foursquare than on Facebook and via Newsletter. Based on this fact, it makes sense to set a clear hierarchy and tie into a standardized distribution schedule. Here is one example:

- ✓ <u>Monthly</u> - Send a Newsletter (which is also posted with a link on your Facebook page)
- ✓ <u>Bi-Weekly</u> - Write a blog post (which is also posted with a link on your Facebook page)
- ✓ <u>Weekly</u> - Post additional content on your Facebook page which is then automatically connected to Twitter, Instagram, etc.
- ✓ <u>Daily</u> - Choose to do additional postings on e.g., Twitter, Instagram, Foursquare or other, but don't choose to redirect them all to Facebook to avoid spamming your "fans" over and over.

Do you remember ASM (A Small World)? Or Myspace? Or Google Buzz? These are all real examples of sites with similar potential as Facebook which had their "rise and fall" cycles. Right now, there is a growing trend that the most active young Facebook users are abandoning the platform in favor of Instagram. Nobody knows how this will develop over time in this fast-moving dynamic industry. But it is clear that you need to stay up-to-date with the latest trends if you are going to reap the fruits of future opportunities that will ultimately be available.

<u>Tip #35: Stay tuned on the fast changing Social Media trends</u>

One particularly excellent resource to stay up-to-date with the latest social media and other technology trends is <u>mashable.com</u>. Follow their trending stories on a weekly basis. I have been able to stay in-the-know and have been inspired to test new online tools and tricks long before discovered by competition.

Online ads

The phrase "online ads" refers to all links to your website (text or graphical) placed on an external website to whom you are paying for the ad space. There are various payment models for this including, fixed fee/month, fixed fee/ thousand views, cost per click, cost per conversion or commission on sales.

There are basically two ways to buy online ads:

1.   Directly from the site owner
2.   Indirectly, via an intermediary

In the first case, it is easy to start thinking of broadcast media, such as newspaper websites. It is true that these have by far the largest audience, but they are also an expensive marketing choice. If you don't run a large scale company, it is typically better to find content sites related to your niche of business.

Tip #36: Evaluate potential direct ad partners for your niche

Remember that this traffic has dual benefits (hot traffic and links), so consider both, when you decide which niche site to place an ad on and what you are willing to pay:

1. To maximize the "hot traffic" - Place the ad on websites where your potential customers might hang out, optimally when they would be in the buying mode for your product /service

2. To get quality links to build Page Rank - Place your ad on a content site that has high Page Rank, but a low number of outgoing links, to help build your Page Rank (as discussed in chapter 2). Ideally the ad should not be recognized by Google as a paid ad , but appear as a natural link, since this gives better page authority.

When considering indirect purchase of ads, you have several options to consider, but the quickest and most common is to activate the Display ad Network in Google Adwords.

Remember that it has some severe pitfalls (as discussed in Tip #9.) Take a very cautious approach.

Tip #37: Experiment with Google display network, but be cautious

The cautious technique is to carefully screen out the real (value adding sites) from the spam sites, and then allow Google to only place your ads on these content sites that have been approved by you. Google AdSense has a network of over a million sites (display partners), and it also includes specific Google sites such as Gmail and YouTube, so the key is to find the handful that actually are valuable for you.

You can do this by:

1. Start by allowing your ads to occur on all sites (that contain the keywords you are targeting.)
2. Doing daily (or even hourly checks) to block sites which drive a lot of clicks without generating any conversions.
3. Following this closely you can probably screen out a handful of websites that have some value for you. This would typically be some niche content sites (as discussed earlier in this chapter.)
4. Later on you might also consider to buy ads directly from these niche content websites

Besides finding the good niche sites, the above approach will also show you if it is worth it to keep your ads appearing in high ranking platforms such as Gmail and YouTube. In the case of unitedsurfcamps.com it proved not to be worth it as a general ad display. But for remarketing campaigns, as discussed in Tip #10, it proved profitable.

I also strongly recommend having separate bids and budgets on Google AdWords for your search networks campaigns and your display network campaigns. Because search traffic is typically "hotter," you may be willing to pay a higher CPC for it in order to meet your max. cost/conversion.

Besides Google, there are several other "wholesalers" of ad space on numerous networks. Some of them offer different business models than CPC, called affiliate marketing. It is based on commission for actual conversions to the site owners.

Tip #38: Evaluate potential use of affiliate marketing networks

The most important affiliate marketing platforms internationally are Commission Junction, LinkShare.com and Tradedoubler.com. There are also many local and niched affiliate marketing networks to be explored.

During recent years the large affiliate marketing networks have increased their offerings to overlap more and more with other online marketing offers, for example, regular ads (pay per click) and e-mail marketing. So be sure to sort out exactly what you want to join (and not) before engaging.

Another interesting development is "deal of the day" platforms, such as Groupon that reach out to a large audience of subscribers.

Tip #39: Evaluate potential use of Groupon or similar "deal of the day" programs

Groupon and similar programs can be an attractive way to reach new customers. However, note that it typically requires you to offer a huge discount, meaning that you need to be very careful when evaluating the business case so you don't end up losing more money than you gain.

It will typically be more attractive if you have:

1. High gross margin share (e.g. 80%) on your products (e.g. luxury products or digital products)
2. Excess merchandize in stock to put on sale
3. Available space (e.g., hotel rooms) which you will not be able to book

4. Products that will be purchased frequently if the first time user likes them (e.g., socks)
5. A subscription business model (e.g., gym membership) and can "hook" the users after the first try

Another important development is the evolution of "comparison shopping engines" such as PriceGrabber and Nextag. The basic functionality of comparison shopping engines is to:

1. Collect product information, including pricing, from participating e-commerce sites
2. Display that collective information on a single results page in response to a shopper's search query
3. Enable shoppers to compare each retailer's price, shipping options, and service on a single page and choose the one which offers the best overall value

Tip #40: Evaluate potential use of comparison shopping engines

Adding your website (if applicable) to different comparison shopping engines enables you to list your product offers on the comparison site and pay per click (CPC) for the "hot traffic" it generates. The obvious downside to this (from the seller's perspective) is a very hard price pressure. So this mainly makes sense if you are able to compete on prices.

So far comparison shopping engines have mainly been applied for commodity e-commerce products. But there is a growing evolution of comparison engines that target a specific niche (e.g. insuremytrip.com, comparetextbooks.net, rentalcars.com).

"Offline" marketing

With "offline" marketing I mean all kinds of traditional marketing channels which you cannot "click" on. This includes Direct mail, Flyers, Newspapers, Magazines, Radio and TV.

Even though you cannot technically click on the "offline" ad or article, you can still use some smart techniques to track conversions anyway.

Tip #41: Apply conversion trackers also for "offline marketing"

For example, you can display a coupon or "special offer" with a unique redemption code in the advertisement and then track how many times it is being used. This way you can calculate your cost/conversion also for "offline" media channel, and you can compare and analyze what is the most profitable marketing mix for you such as Paid Search vs. online ads vs. offline ads, etc.

Another example is to include a QR-code in the "offline" ad, enabling the user to take a photo with his smartphone and to be redirected to your landing page (with a tracking code from the ad he was directed from.)

"Offline" marketing typically works best for companies that address a local market such as a certain country or a city. For example, I have seen this work quite well for a local company that distributes flyers with the website name and redemption code that is traceable.

"Offline" marketing can also work well for building brand recognition locally, meaning that people who could be future customers will have you in mind when they eventually consider to buy what you offer. An indication of this is when you get a big share of direct traffic, people writing your website address directly in the browser. You will also see increased search traffic where your brand name is the keyword.

Summary

In summary, Social Media is a very dynamic environment. But you can manage it effectively by using Facebook as the "motor" and automatically connect your Facebook stream to other channels.

Unlike using Google AdWords, SEO and having a Facebook page, online ads are not something that every online business should apply broadly. The marketing mix of "online ad options" will heavily depend on your business logic and the ongoing trends you are able to discover and monetize.

Remember that non-search traffic has a dual effect:

1. To generate direct "hot traffic" which may make a transaction at your landing page
2. To generate links that will boost your Page Rank in organic search

When buying ads, you should evaluate both these benefits. Finally, remember to "think online" also when you are purchasing traditional "offline" media.

Practical tips presented in this chapter:

Tip #32: Use Facebook ads to build a critical mass of likes on your Facebook page

Tip #33: Use Facebook both as a marketing channel and customer service channel

Tip #34: Synergize Facebook with other social media channels

Tip #35: Stay tuned to the fast changing Social Media trends

Tip #36: Evaluate potential direct ad partners for your niche

Tip #37: Experiment with Google display network, but be very cautious

Tip #38: Evaluate potential use of affiliate marketing networks

Tip #39: Evaluate potential use of Groupon or similar "deal of the day" programs

Tip #40: Evaluate potential use of comparison shopping engines

Tip #41: Apply conversion trackers also for "offline marketing"

Resources mentioned in chapter 3

Social Media Platforms (other than Facebook):

✓ **Twitter** (twitter.com) - Social media platform that allows max. 140 symbol messages.
✓ **Instagram** (instagram.com) - Social media platform centered on sharing photos.

✓ **Foursquare** (foursquare.com) - Social media platform focused on location tagging such as tagging in your office / cafe / holiday destination) and sharing with your friends.

Information on new Social Media trends:

✓ **Mashable** (mashable.com) - Probably the best global resource to stay tuned with new trends in Social Media and other information technology.

Other Non-Search Traffic Sources:

✓ **Google Display Network** (google.pl/ads/displaynetwork) - The quickest and most common platform for indirect purchase of ads.
✓ **Affiliate marketing platforms** (CJ.com; LinkShare.com and Tradedoubler.com).
✓ **"Deal of the day" platforms** (e.g., groupon.com, appsumo.com).
✓ **Comparison shopping engines** (PriceGrabber.com and Nextag.com).

CHAPTER 4

Successfully convert traffic into customers

Introduction - The three step approach to maximize your conversion rates

In the previous three chapters, we have discussed how to generate traffic ("paid search," "organic search" and "non-search") to your website. But this traffic is of little use unless you can "monetize" it and generate an income (or other benefit.)

We previously defined "hot traffic" as visitors coming to your site that are likely to make a conversion, while "cold traffic" are visitors you cannot monetize.

A key performance indicator to measure this is conversion rate, which is defined as:

Number of conversions/ number of visitors

For example, if your conversion rate is 2%, it means that for every 100 visitors you make on average 2 sales.

Working with this part of the business is often referred to as **CRO - Conversion Rate Optimization**. In general you can see this as a three step approach:

1. <u>Build trust</u> – How to make sure the potential customer feels comfortable to work with you?
2. <u>Rig the sales funnel</u> – How to actively lead the visitor into making a conversion?
3. <u>Manage the bouncers</u> – How to handle visitors "falling out" of the sales funnel and to continuously improve conversion rates by effectively analyzing data?

Build trust

Building trust is about convincing a potential client to think, *This is a serious company. I am opened to work with them.*

"Online trust" has many components, but the first one you tend to notice is the web design of the website you visit. If the design feels "tacky," you immediately feel a subconscious hesitation about engaging with this company. Classic mistakes are:

✓ Too much text
✓ Text in many different font sizes
✓ Non-readable text
✓ Unclear structure
✓ Too intense color scales
✓ Moving objects or sounds
✓ Poor explanation of website topic

How to make a successful web design is a science of its own that I will not cover fully in this book. Most likely you would hire a web designer to make a few suggestions for you. Just remember to not let the "creative part" of web design go too far. The main purpose of each landing page is to make the visitor make a conversion, which calls for a simplistic design.

Tip #42: Use a simplistic but modern web design

So, let's say that the website which you are visiting looks nice and trustworthy at first glance. What is the next thing you ask yourself if you have never seen this company before? You probably ask yourself, who this company is? Where do they come from? Why do they do this? What are people saying about them?

Therefore a very important part (which is often overlooked) is to explain (in a credible way) who you are and _why_ you have this website, which is typically done in an "about us"-section on the website.

This is also something that is changing over time. When we started unitedsurfcamps.com in 2005, the key factor was to build a "serious" image, meaning to give a clear impression that "we are a big established company who will not trick you." This is still valid but with increased maturity of online consumers, it has changed. Now, a key factor is to tell the story of where you come from and why you do this. This is because people in general don't believe in what you sell, but _why_ you sell it. See this TED talk for an inspiring lecture on this subject. It is also connected to the growing trend of sustainability/CSR, meaning your customers ask themselves what is your wider contribution to the world (beyond personal profits).

Tip #43: Sell a serious AND personal "story", which shows the people behind the scenes

It can hence be a great benefit to "personalize" your company and present "the people behind the scenes." What is their story, why do they do this, and what are they truly passionate about?

Another important factor in building trust is that you cannot be "best in every aspect." It is instead recommended to clearly formulate and communicate what is your specific "value proposition."

A "value proposition" is a formulation of the main reasons why a potential customer should purchase something from you (instead from a competitor.)

Tip #44: Clearly communicate your "value proposition"

Here is an example of how the value proposition of unitedsurfcamps.com is formulated and communicated on the top domain.

Note that your "value proposition" will not fit everyone. For example, if you have "best quality" and "great experience" as propositions, you will most likely not also have "lowest price" and cater to the "budget segment" of the markets.

Segmenting your market and formulating a value proposition is one of the core concepts taught in all basic marketing courses, and you can easily find lots of further reading about this online.

Another important factor a potential customer should consider is if this is an established and "tested company." Showing customers' testimonials is the best way to meet these criteria (discussed in Tip #50.)

1 Best value for money

Only the top surf camp in each surf zone is accepted membership in United Surf Camps network. Every surf camp fulfill highest quality standards and is regularly evaluated. ▶ Read More

2 Flexible booking conditions

Arrive any day of the week and stay as long as you like. Only 15% deposit needed to make a booking. The deposit is 100% refundable up to 15 days prior to arrival.
▶ Read More

3 Responsible surf travel

Your surf camp stay will also have a wider positive impact, trough our work with Surf safety, Ocean and Beach preservation, Carbon neutral travel and Community investments.
▶ Read More

There is also a clear synergy having a successful Facebook page to support the recommended criteria. Facebook is (so far) a well-known and trusted platform. Having many likes, good content and customer dialogues on your Facebook page will build trust and credibility in your prospects' eyes.

A "dead" Facebook page with very few likes and no interaction is more of a liability, as it would make potential customer suspicious. But an active Facebook page with thousands of followers tells the potential customer that you run a serious business.

Tip #45: Thousands of Facebook likes can't be wrong - show it off

Once you have reached "critical mass" with your Facebook page, you can emphasize this on your website, by integrating Facebook Social plug-ins, telling how many likes you have or what the latest post is about - directly on your website.

A final factor to build trust is to use different external certificates. You can use companies that offer secure SSL encryption (e.g., GeoTrust) or payment providers' endorsements (verified by Visa, MasterCard Secure Code, etc.) There are also a number of (often national) industry organizations that offer memberships and validation logos on your website (with a "click to validate" function.)

Tip #46: Use external certificates to signal trustworthiness

These kinds of certificates used to be a differential factor in the early days of e-commerce. However, over time as the online market space has emerged and evolved, they have become standards. Therefore, you don't need to "show them off" anymore as I (and many others) have in the past.

In summary, building trust is a key component to set a proper "arena" for enabling conversion. To earn the trust of new customers (even if you are not a Fortune 500 company with indisputable brand recognition) you need to:

✓ Have a trustworthy web design
✓ Sell your story
✓ Show that you have lots of customers

Rig the sales funnel

Once you have "the arena of trust" in place, the potential customer feels comfortable enough to keep engaging with your website and is more likely to consider a conversion. To maximize the probability that the conversion will take place, you need to set up an optimal "sales funnel."

The Sales funnel is a combination of the process-steps that a customer will complete upon entering your website, to make a decision that eventually generates an income for you.

Your sales funnel will look different depending on the business model of your website.

✓ If you sell a product or a service, the sales funnel typically ends with the customer taking out his credit card and clicking "pay."

✓ If you are selling leads, it would typically end with the customer leaving your site via clicking on a link to another website where a transaction might take place later.

✓ If you sell premium content, the sales funnel might end with a visitor signing up as a member.

In many cases, you would have a mixed business model that sells both products and leads. Or you might be working in a "freemium model", where:

1. Your first funnel is about signing up members (for free)
2. Later on you have process for upgrading these members to become paying customers

In order to make your sales funnel a successful reality, you need to clearly define your "business model hierarchy."

Tip #47: Nail your business model hierarchy

For example, if you can make the most money selling one type of products directly on the site, you do not want to dilute this by including lots of sponsored links (selling leads) in the center of the page. But if you can guide the visitor through the site and share some benefits (e.g., selling leads) with the clients who don't buy your core service, it can prove beneficial.

Knowing your "business model hierarchy" is a key success factor to design conversion-friendly websites. In order to get "there," you should:

1. Write down the "objective" of each landing page (what action you want the visitor to take.)
2. Optimize each landing page to make it "click-friendly" mainly for the action(s) you want the visitor to take.

Tip #48: Make each landing page "conversion friendly"

As an example, study this print screen from a landing page at unitedsurfcamps.com

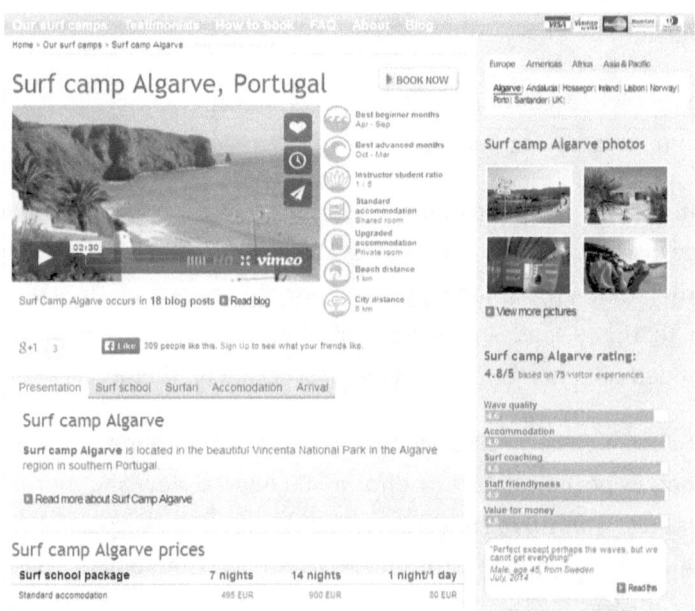

Note everything that has a distinct red color is an action I want the visitor to take. The smaller actions ("Read more", Read blog", View more pictures," etc.) are about convincing the visitor to complete a booking. Note the largest and most distinct action button is "BOOK NOW" which will lead the visitor to the next step of the sales funnel. The "BOOK NOW" button also appears again at the bottom of the page.

Finding the best design to maximize conversions requires a lot of testing and iteration. You can use A/B-test for this, meaning that you set up two different designs and then split your incoming traffic 50/50 to conclude which design is the most effective. This is the same principle as previously discussed in Tip #5 (for testing different ad designs.)

The above picture also demonstrates another best practice: make us of "enriched content" to convince the potential customer to make a conversion.

With "enriched content" I mean all graphical elements (not purely text, i.e., photos and movies.)

When it comes to photos, it is important to have big enough photos so the visitor can get a true feeling about what the photo is "selling." In order to keep the loading time short (discussed in Tip #28), it is wise to firstly load small icons of the photos only. They can be expanded on visitor's request (e.g., by clicking on them.

If you sell a physical product, you can offer an extreme "zoom-in" of the details of the product or offer a 360 degree view and more likely experience a positive conversion. This practice has successfully been introduced by friends of mine running the online business tailorcut.com.

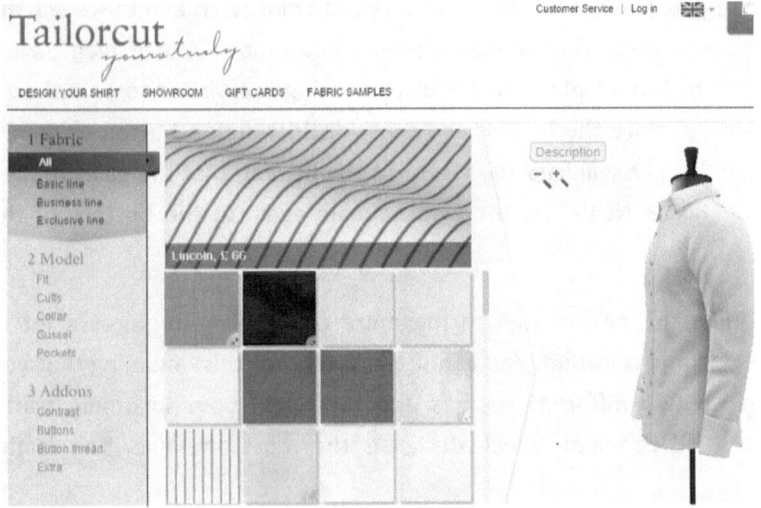

Here you design your own shirt and see a rotating 3D-model of the shirt as you change design and fabrics. To get a genuine feeling of the fabric, you can see an extreme close-up picture. Of course, it is not exactly the same as touching it, but it gives you a profound understanding of the quality and texture anyway.

Next, consider the fact that photos of real people who are happy and smiling tend to drive better conversion than photos without people. According to research, it is the "positive feeling" around your product or service, that drive sales[12].

Videos are another great way to create a "positive feeling" and to further let the customers experience the product or service you are offering. In the case of unitedsurfcamps.com, we were able to increase the conversion rate by 20% after including a video presentation of each surf camp.

Tip #49: Use enriched content (photos, video etc.) to create a positive feeling"

One of the most effective factors to convince a potential buyer is to show ratings and testimonials from previous customers. This can be achieved either by your own system or using a third party when applicable (e.g., TripAdvisor.com if you sell accommodation) or both.

Best practice Tip #50: Use testimonials and other endorsements for your products

If you have your own system, it is important that you stick to ethics and present ratings from all clients (not only the satisfied ones).

---

[12] e.g. marketingexperiments.com/blog/general/stock-images-tested.html

Research[13] has even shown that a product with mainly positive but some negative ratings actually drive higher conversions than products with only positive ratings. Products with only positive ratings make customers suspicious.

Remember that these customer evaluations also can be marked with "rich snippets" to be shown directly in Google's search result (as discussed in Tip #31.)

An effective way to build and improve each step of the sales funnel is to ask yourself, *What questions might I have as a customer right now that makes me hesitant to continue?*

By anticipating this and providing the answers to questions like these proactively, you can effectively continue to lead the visitor through the sales funnel.

Tip #51: Offer proactive answers to potential questions

If you are not successful with this, you will typically have many visitors that "bounce" (leaving the sales funnel) either to contact you or to move on to a competitor's site.

How to anticipate these questions?

- ✓ Analyze what questions you receive from customers contacting you
- ✓ Benchmark you competitors' sales funnels

A common behavior of visitors is that they first "window shop" and then come back later to make a transaction. This would not really be a problem if they always come back to your website, but since the

---

[13] unbounce.com/conversion-rate-optimization/customer-reviews-conversion-rates/

barriers on Internet are so low the risk is that they will end up somewhere else.

One way to manage this is to use Google AdWords' "remarketing campaigns" (as discussed in Tip #10.) But it is even more attractive if you can convince a customer to make the transaction rather now, than later. This is something you can affect by using "scarcity reminders."

Tip #52: Use scarcity reminders to avoid window shopping

Scarcity means that a product or service will not always be available, at least not for the same price. There are four main types of scarcity arguments you can use:

1. Limited quantities - Inform the visitor that you are offering a limited number of units for sale (or have limited in stock.)
2. Price increase - Inform the visitor that the price will likely go up in the near future.
3. Price decrease - Inform the visitor that a discount or special promotion will end in the near future.
4. Deadlines - Inform the visitor that the offer is only valid for a limited period of time

Another crucial metric (besides conversion rate) is the income/ conversion. To improve this metric, you need to stimulate the visitor to buy more things from you than he had in mind when entering your site.

The key factor to stimulate customers to "fill-up the shopping basket" is to make sure that your site's offerings are easily navigated among.

A common pitfall is to force a customer to go back into site hierarchy to the start-page or "main assortment page" to check out another of your offerings. It is instead a proven tip to have direct links between your landing pages with a pedagogic "tracker" showing where you are. If you sell a large range of products in different categories they can be grouped together (as in example picture below).

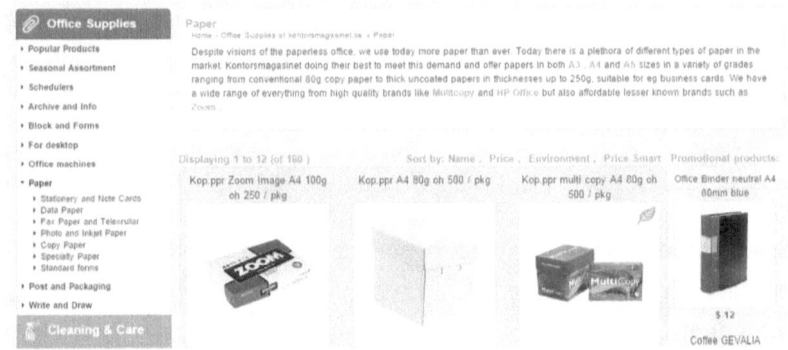

This picture is from the website kontorsmagasinet.se which sells office supplies on the Swedish market (and was founded by friends of mine). By having the left navigation bar always tracking the user in three levels of "category hierarchy," it enables quick navigation among the thousands of products they offer.

Tip #53: Have direct navigation between your offerings

Another way to stimulate the customers to buy more is to add incentives connected to volumes. A proven example tactic is to offer free delivery over a certain purchase value. This makes sense (for physical products) since you typically have a (almost) fixed cost of delivery which cannot be covered by your margin for small purchases. But if the customer is buying a lot it is a "win-win" that the delivery is included.

Tip #54: Stimulate batch buying (e.g. offer free delivery above a certain purchase value)

Another way to maximize income/conversion is through "up-selling", meaning that you stimulate the visitor to add additional products in his "shopping basket" before checking out.

Tip #55: Up-sell relevant products in the right moment

One effective way to do this is to use a recommendation module informing the visitor that "Customers who bought this also bought…".

Another way is to automatically recommend "add-on" services at the end of the sales funnel. This is, for example, common for travel insurance when you are booking a flight online.

Just note that there can be a fine borderline between getting additional income from up-selling vs. making the customer irritated and bouncing (no conversion). If you are not a budget player but rather have a premium value proposition you need to be very careful, so you keep your promises.

Once a visitor commits to a conversion the key success factor (besides up-selling) is to make the check-out process as quick and smooth as possible.

If the customer experiences "hassle" in your check-out process you risk that he "bounces" and the sale is lost. The hassle might be out of your control, i.e. if their internet connection is lost or if they receive an incoming phone call and forget about you. It is in your favor to make sure the check-out is quick.

Tip #56: Simplify the check-out process

A few examples of how you can simplify the check-out process are:

1. Have as few steps as possible - Each time you ask the customer to click on "next step" you risk that he will bounce (e.g., if the next step doesn't load correctly due to an issue beyond your control).
2. Simplify data collection - Avoid demanding data (e.g., personal information) before you actually need it, and question only if you really need it. For example you don't need a person's name and nationality to present them a price offer.
3. Avoid mandatory membership - One common mistake is that you might be asked to either "log-in" or "create an account" before checking out. This is a big "bounce factor" and something you should try to avoid. It is instead better to do this more discretely and recommend the customer in the final step (after conversion) if they also want to set-up an account for future purchases.
4. Offer log-in with Facebook or Google - If you have a business model that really calls for making the customers "create an account", one of the best ways to do this is by using a plug-in from Facebook and/or Google which automatically creates the account.

A final factor to avoid bouncing is to offer a wide range of payment options. If the customer cannot pay for your product (if that is your business model) all previous marketing and sales efforts are lost.

Today most advanced Internet users have a credit card, and if you offer payments with VISA and MasterCard your will reach the vast majority of Internet users.

However, note that there are many national variations to this. For example, American Express and Diners have quite large market shares in the USA. In Germany, Denmark and several other countries there are "domestic cards" that have large market shares.

The most important for you is:

✓ To fulfill the expectations of your customers and hence offer payment methods that they can use.
✓ Consider if having better a more payment options than your competitors can be a part of your value proposition.

Tip #57: Offer multiple Payment possibilities

Here is a general overview of the most common payment options:

1. <u>Integrated credit card solution</u> - In this case you work with a payment service provider (e.g., DIBS or AYDEN) that hook you up directly with credit card payments as a customized fully integrated part of your sales funnel.
2. <u>Electronic wallets (e.g., PayPal)</u> - This is the quickest and simplest way to get a payment option "semi-integrated" at your website. The downside with PayPal and other electronic wallets is that they charge a higher commission than integrated payment service providers (e.g., 5% instead of 2%) and have a limited flexibility for integration at your website.
3. <u>Direct bank transfer</u> - For customers that don't have a credit card this can be a good option. It also means lower commission fees, since you get the money directly. The downside is that you need to set up a direct link with banks on each local market.
4. <u>Invoice</u> - You can always offer an invoice which customers can pay later (e.g., via their Internet bank). However, you are exposed to a credit risk, meaning a risk that the customer will not pay the invoice. One way to come around this is to use the services offered by <u>Klarna.com</u> and similar players. They will

handle the invoicing and money collection for you and instead pay you directly (although with a high commission.)

5. <u>Other</u> - There are many payment options evolving (e.g., SMS-payments) so stay tuned on the latest trends to see if there might be an opportunity for you.

Manage the bouncers

To optimize the conversion rate you need to understand the behavior of your visitors who do NOT convert. The first thing to understand is where in the sales funnel they are "bouncing". The good news is that this can easily be done (for free!) using <u>Google Analytics</u>.

In the behavior-section of Google Analytics you can:

✓ Track how visitors are moving around on your website
✓ See what events they are performing
✓ See where they are leaving your site
✓ Compare the bounce rate % and exit % for each of your landing pages

For example in the picture below, Google Analytics shows (in a visually smart way) where visitors click after they enter the top-domain of unitedsurfcamps.com.

If you have an integrated search field on your website, you can also get valuable statistics on what people are searching for (and not) and how they behave after the search. This can be very valuable input to further optimization of your landing pages and to discover additional keywords and business opportunities.

In the conversions-section of Google Analytics, you can visualize your sales funnel and define goals for each step. You can then track the actual conversion rate in relation to the goals.

Based on this insight, you can conduct A/B-tests with different designs of your landing pages. This can be tracked directly in the Behavior >Experiment-section in Google Analytics.

Tip #58: Use Google Analytics for continuous improvements of conversions

Google Analytics is also the ultimate place to see exact traffic statistics (e.g. organic vs. inorganic search.) You can also explore the different web browsers (Chrome, Safari, Firefox, Explorer etc.) your visitors are using. By tracking the behavior flow per web browser you might also discover potential issues which are technology related (e.g., high bounce rate for one browser on one specific page.)

Focusing on one web browser is a common pitfall in web design. You will be surprised to see how different your website might look in another browser. Therefore, it is important to test the website performance in many browsers as a "quality assurance."

Tip #59: Ensure user-friendliness for all browsers (Chrome, Safari, Firefox, Explorer etc.)

Besides different browsers you also need to test and investigate how your website is being perceived on different platforms (Smartphones, Tablets, and Computers.)

The good news is that by using **responsive website design**, you can code your website to work well on any device (desktop, tablet, mobile phones with different screen sets) without creating multiple versions of your website.

Tip #60: Ensure user friendliness for all platforms (Mobile phones, Tablets, Computers)

There are several tools available online which can evaluate how user-friendly your website is on different platforms and give you suggestions of updates. On e.g., mobiletest.me you can even see how your website looks on different kind of models of smartphones and tablets.

While your visitors are interacting with your website, technical issues will inevitably occur. Some of them are due to external factors, for example, a problem with your web-hotel or the visitor's Internet connection. Others will be "internal", meaning that there is an issue in the code of your website which can be fixed.

One issue that can be both internal and external is "broken links." If this occurs, your visitors are being directed to a place on your website which does not exist. In this case your browser will show a "404 error page" telling you that the site does not seem to exist.

To prevent the visitor from "bouncing" completely, i.e., leaving your site for good, you can instead show a customized error page, with links back to your most important landing pages.

Tip #61: Customize your 404 error page

A successful tactic can be to include a portion of humor to your customized 404 page, which will make your visitor more tolerant towards the error.

There are many good examples of customized 404 pages to be found online. For example you can check out https://creativemarket.com/blog/2013/07/22/the-best-404-pages-on-the-internet.

Summary

In summary, the ability to successfully convert traffic into customers is equally important as traffic generation. These two are also interconnected. If you acquire new traffic that is "cold," your conversion rate will go down even if your website and offering are the same.

The conversion rate can also be affected by external factors like changes in competitors' offerings, price sensitivity of customers and other trends. So it is important to constantly monitor this and understand what are the internal vs. external factors.

From the macro point of view, the "internal factors" can be optimized by first building an "arena" of trust and inspiration, making sure that the potential customers feel comfortable and passionate about making business with you. Secondly it is all about setting and continuously improving the sales funnel. These two combined will maximize the conversion rate and the sales/ conversion metrics.

Practical tips presented in this chapter:

Tip #42: Use a simplistic but modern web design

Tip #43: Sell a serious put personal "story" and show the people behind

Tip #44: Clearly communicate your "value proposition"

Tip #45: Thousands of Facebook likes can't be wrong - show it off

Tip #46: Use external certificates to signal trustworthiness

Tip #47: Nail your business model hierarchy

Tip #48: Make each landing page "conversion friendly"

Tip #49: Use enriched content (photos, video etc.) to create a positive feeling"

Tip #50: Use testimonials and other endorsements for your products

Tip #51: Offer proactive answers to potential questions

Tip #52: Use scarcity reminders to avoid window shopping

Tip #53: Have direct navigation between your offerings

Tip #54: Stimulate batch buying (e.g., offer free delivery over a certain purchase value)

Tip #55: Up-sell relevant products in the right moment

Tip #56: Simplify the check-out process

Tip #57: Offer multiple Payment possibilities

Tip #58: Use Google Analytics for continuous improvements of conversions

Tip #59: Ensure user-friendliness for all browsers (Chrome, Safari, Firefox, Explorer, etc.)

Tip #60: Ensure user-friendliness for all platforms (Mobile phones, Tablets, Computers)

Tip #61: Customize your 404 error page

Resources mentioned in chapter 4

<u>Webpage Analysis / Testing:</u>

✓ **Google Analytics** (google.com/analytics) - The best free tool available for improving your website performance. Gives insights of where your traffic is coming from and how it is behaving on your website. It also enables you to conduct A/B-tests (e.g., different designs of your landing pages) in the Behavior >Experiment-section.

✓ **Testing different platforms / devices** (e.g., mobiletest.me)

<u>Payment Methods and Services Related:</u>

✓ **Electronic wallets** - (E.g., paypal.com)

✓ **Payment Service providers** - (E.g., dibspayment.com/ or adyen.com)- Lower commission than electronic wallets

✓ **Outsourced invoice handling and collection** - (E.g., klarna.com)- get invoices paid quicker and with less hassle

CHAPTER 5

Maximize the value from your customer base

Introduction - The three hidden values of your customer base

In the previous chapter, we discussed how to convert the traffic on your website into "first-time" customers. However, this is only a portion of the total benefits your customer base can bring you.

In this chapter we will discuss how to maximize the total value of these customers, after the first purchase. This can be summarized in three main opportunities:

1. Stimulate your customer to make another purchase from you
2. Associate other business opportunities with your customer base
3. Let your customers sell for you

Stimulate your customer to make another purchase from you

How many times during a life time could a customer consider buying from you? The answer obviously depends on the type of product/service you are offering. If you are selling wedding dresses, a typical customer will only use your service once. On the other hand, if you are selling food or other consumables, your customer might buy from you every week.

It means that:

- ✓ During a period of 10 years, a customer who buys a weekly product would make 52 x10 = 520 purchases.
- ✓ This hence means that the first purchase they made is only 1/520 = 0,2% of the total value of this customer.
- ✓ By stimulating the customer to do repeat sales from you (and not switch to a competitor) you can hence secure the remaining 99.8% of the total value.

One of the most straightforward ways to do this is to offer discounts to loyal customers. If the customers, for example, know that they have a 10% discount on all future purchases from you, they have less incentive to switch to a competitor. This 10% will of course be taken from you margin. For this to make sense your margin needs to be well above the discount percent.

Tip #62: Drive re-purchase via loyalty discounts

For products or services less frequently needed, the customer might need to be reminded and inspired to make another purchase. A great way to do this is by sending newsletters to your customer base.

To convert recipients of the newsletters into sales, you need to make the newsletter "conversion-friendly." It is the same logic as when optimizing your landing pages for conversion. You need to have a clear hierarchy on where you want the customers to click in the newsletter and send them to a landing page where they can make a conversion.

Tip #63: Use conversion optimized newsletters to get your customers back to the site

There are many newsletter campaign platforms (e.g., mailchimp.com) that offer cost effective management of newsletter campaigns. A key feature is that they use tracking codes in the mails enabling you to see:

✓ How many people opened and read the e-mail
✓ How many people clicked on a link in the newsletter
✓ Which person clicked what particular link
✓ How they further interacted with your website after the click

Once you have more than 1000 newsletter subscribers, it can be worth it to run the A/B test on the design of the newsletter on a smaller group (e.g, 100 subscribers) before sending it out to the wider audience. This is the same concept as discussed in tip #5 and in tip #66.

If you reach over 10,000 subscribers, you can also consider to segment your newsletter based on your customer characteristics. There are three main ways to segment the newsletter:

1. Demographics (age, gender, native language, place of living, etc.)
2. Likely purchase patterns (interest, previous sales, etc.)
3. Online attention – meaning how often they think it is OK (and NOT OK) to receive newsletters

Tip #64: Segment the newsletter, to minimize unsubscribing

For example, let's say you are selling sports shoes online.

Using the first example (demographics), you can customize your e-mail campaign and only send female shoe offerings to your female customers (and vice versa.)

Using the second example (purchase patterns), you might have insights that one customer group is particularly interested in tennis shoes (neither running, nor trekking.) Then you can customize a campaign only focused on tennis to them.

In the third example (online attention), you ask your customers how often they want to receive e-mails from you and include them in e-mail campaigns based on their preferred frequency. You can consider to first include them in the high-frequency category but then after clicking on the "unsubscribe"-link in the newsletter, try to move them down in frequency, rather than doing a full exit. You can also ask the customers why they want to unsubscribe, to give you valuable feedback on how to design future campaigns.

By making smart segmentation of your newsletter, you will provide your customer base with the most interesting information for them, on their chosen terms. Which will hence minimize the "unsubscribing" and stimulate loyalty.

Another best practice relating to newsletters is to always strive to personalize the interactions you have with your customers. An example of this is to start the newsletter with the customer's name. For example, a most acceptable greeting might be "Dear Caroline" instead of "Dear customer." This is an automated feature provided by most newsletter platforms. In the same way an e-mail can be personally written and signed by a real sender (not by "the company.")

Tip #65: Personalize the interactions with your customers

To maximize the value of the newsletter, you need to catch your subscribers' attention and inspire them. To make optimal "copy-writing" is a science of its own which I will not go into detail in this book. Besides personalizing the communication, key features include how to:

✓ Set eye-catching headlines
✓ Tell a credible story
✓ Focus on the customer needs (rather than your products)

There are several interesting articles and courses in effective copy-writing available online. One particular inspiring one is appsumo.com/copywriting-course/.

Another way to stimulate repeat sales is to make it easy for your customers to log-in when they return to your website. This can be done either with cookies, tracking code in the link of a newsletter or IP recognition. It does not mean that you will be automatically logged-in, but the username can be pre-filled and the site can be shown in the right language format, showing previous viewed products, etc.

Tip #66: Simplify the log-in for repeat customers

If you have the log-in connected to Facebook or Google (as discussed in tip #56), it also simplifies the process.

Associate other business opportunities with your customer base

Besides selling the "same" products to your customers repeatedly you can also sell them other things (not your core business) based on your insights about them.

Using the example of sport shoes again you can for example set-up directed campaigns for:

✓ Tennis rackets - to customers who have previously purchased tennis shoes
✓ Trekking trips - to your customers who have previously purchased trekking shoes
✓ Running competition signups - to customers who have previously purchased running shoes

It does not mean that you necessarily need to expand your own assortment. Instead you can offer associating products via partnerships. This way you can become an "affiliate marketer" who sells "leads." You can either set up a business model where you get paid per click or get a commission, for example 5% on all sales completed by "your" customer on the partner's site.

Tip #67: Offer associating products from partners to your customers (selling leads)

The way to approach this is to deeply think through and recognize the value your customer insights could be to other parties.

Let your customers sell for you

We previously discussed how you can maximize the value of your customer base either by buying more things directly from you, or indirectly by selling leads to partners who would benefit from reaching your customers.

The third way to get additional value from your customer base is to use your current customers to gain new customers for you.

An effective way to do this is to ask your customers for evaluations and endorsements of your products and you as a company. By showing both the quantitative ratings (e.g., on scale 1-5) for each product and some written testimonials, you build trust and will increase the conversion rate of the rated products (as discussed in chapter 4.)

These evaluations can also be tagged with "rich snippets" (as discussed in tip #31) increasing "clickability" and your organic search traffic.

Tip #68: Ask your customers for evaluations and endorsements

Since a customer evaluation is of such big value to you, it is wise to give your customers an incentive to take the time to fill it in. This can also be combined with the loyalty discount previously discussed. For example in the case of unitedsurfcamps.com, we offer all customers who fill in the evaluation form a 5% discount on their next purchase.

Another way to enable your customers to promote your products is to integrate social referral buttons as the last step in the check-out process. This is how it looks at unitedsufcamps.com:

This makes it easy for the customer to share his liking with people in his social networks, who could be new potential customers.

Tip #69: Offer Social Media sharing directly after the purchase

Asking for evaluations and social media sharing is something you can engage every customer in. However, you can go even further with your most passionate customers, asking them to be your "ambassadors."

This means that you, for example, ask for permission to write an article or a blog post about them and their experience with your offering. You can also use them in the customer service process and offer new clients to ask them about tips based on their experience. If they have their own blog, they can promote your products to their followers and get a kick-back on the sale they generate.

If they have potential customers in their network, you can stimulate them to persuade their friends to buy from you. Either with direct kick-backs, e.g. commission on sales, or more subtly by giving them and the people in their network good discounts. This type of activity provides a "win-win-win" situation.

As an example with unitedsurfcamps.com we have successfully used ambassadors to organize surf trips for our customers' friends and student associations. The benefit for the ambassador is that he can join the surf trip for free.

Tip #70: Set up an ambassador program for your most passionate customers

Potential ambassador candidates can easily be screened out by reviewing your customer data. Look for customers who:

- ✓ Buy a lot from you,
- ✓ Write testimonials
- ✓ Make social buzz

They are ideal candidates. If they also have their own blog and/or interesting networks for you to engage with, it is even better.

Summary

In summary, I would argue that most companies have a much bigger potential available among their customer base than they realize. By communicating in a trustworthy way and offering your customer base things they actually desire (but might not know they desire) you can have a life-time win-win relation with your customers.

There is a legendary saying that "the customer is always right", which is true to a large extent. It also means that if you can stimulate your customers to say the "right things" you can let them do business for you.

Remember also to put on the "glasses" of different companies and acknowledge what value your customer base would have to them. Maybe there is even more money in this than in your core business?

Practical tips presented in this chapter:

Tip #62: Drive re-purchase via loyalty discounts

Tip #63: Use conversion optimized newsletters to get your customers back to the site

Tip #64: Segment the newsletter, to minimize unsubscribing

Tip #65: Personalize the interactions with your customers

Tip #66: Simplify the log-in for repeat customers

Tip #67: Offer associating products from partners to your customers (selling leads)

Tip #68: Ask your customers for evaluations and endorsements

Tip #69: Offer Social Media sharing directly after the purchase

Tip #70: Set up an ambassador program for your most passionate customers

Resources mentioned in chapter 5

✓ **Newsletter campaign platforms** (e.g., mailchimp.com)
✓ **Copywriting courses** (e.g., appsumo.com/copywriting-course/

CHAPTER 6

Minimize costs and effort

Introduction - Low cost opportunities in five categories

In previous chapters we discussed how to maximize the revenues from an online business. The key steps included:

✓ Generating traffic
✓ Converting the traffic to first-time customers
✓ Maximizing the value of your customer base

In this chapter we will pursue the cost side of the business. There are five main cost categories in online business to consider:

1. Sales & Marketing - Costs related to generating traffic and building brand recognition
2. Customer Service - Costs related to customer interactions in the sales and aftersales processes
3. Sourcing, Production & Transport - Costs of purchasing, producing, stock-keeping and delivering the products (mainly valid for "physical products")
4. IT & Content Management - Costs for development and management of web solutions and digital content
5. Administration - For example invoice handling, payments handling and accounting.

Fortunately, there are plenty of opportunities to be "street-smart" and minimize both the costs and time needed for each cost category.

Sales & Marketing

Sales & Marketing cost is often the biggest cost for online business, excluding the sourcing costs of the products you sell.

The good news is that everything online can be easily measured and evaluated, which is not the case for offline channels. For example it is very challenging to track how many people who entered a physical store due to a commercial they saw on TV a long time ago.

By including Google Analytics tracking code on your website (as discussed in tip #7 and #58) you can see:

- ✓ How much traffic came to your site during a certain period?
- ✓ What was the source of it (paid search, organic search, social media, referral, etc.)?
- ✓ How did the visitors behave (e.g., made a conversion or not)?

By exporting this data to Excel, you can make your own "controller tool" and include also other marketing metrics.

You can also include your budget and targets, calculate break-even and return on investment for each marketing component. By following this up on a regular basis (e.g., every month) you will get alerts that help you discover whether your business is going in the desired direction or not.

Tip #71: Set up a regular marketing evaluation routine

Note that you can calculate cost per conversion for all media mix including "off-line" (radio, newspaper, TV, flyers, etc.) with some assumptions.

Firstly, marketing evaluation can be tracked with direct means (e.g., using QR codes or traceable coupon-codes). Secondly, it can be tracked by the exclusion method. With exclusion method, I mean that if you make an isolated campaign (e.g., in radio), you can compare how much more sales you probably will have the coming period compared to your baseline. The baseline is the revenue you would have if you did not do the radio campaign. Given that your baseline is only driven by online traffic (and there are no significant changes in the market), you should have a pretty good knowledge of such. As a result, you can then calculate the difference between the actual sales and the baseline as the net effect of the radio campaign.

Let's say that your expected baseline sale (given the traffic your receive) is 1000 conversions in a specific month. But during this month, you conducted a radio campaign and received 1200 conversions. The difference is that 200 conversions (most likely) are connected to your campaign. If you paid $1000 for the radio campaign, your cost per conversion is 1000/200 = $5, which can be compared to your conversion costs for Google Adwords and other channels (as discussed in tip #7.)

Another example is the "conversion-cost" of a loyalty discount. Let's say you are selling products for an average value of $100 and your average gross margin is 20%. Those results mean that your average gross income is $20 / sale. If you give a 10% loyalty discount, the "marketing-cost" for this project will be $10 / conversion, which can be compared to your conversion costs from other initiatives.

<u>Tip #72: Track and calculate cost per conversion for all</u>
<u>media mix, not only online</u>

With more advanced regression analysis it is actually possible to calculate this for multiple campaigns at the same time. This is an offering that consulting firms typically offer large companies which run multiple marketing campaigns at the same time. However, for small and medium enterprises, I would recommend to:

1. Keep it simple
2. Try one campaign at the time
3. Learn and improve gradually

Customer Service

Customer service is all interactions you have with the customers during the sales and the after-sales process. These interactions have big impact on how you are being perceived by your customers and what evaluations they will give you.

The first question you need to ask yourself is what availability your customer service shall have. This is a very strategic question since it affects your value proposition and customer experience.

If your strategy is to differentiate vs. competitors by offering the best availability you might state that "We answer all calls and e-mails within 30 seconds 24/7". To deliver om this promise will require a large scale and costly customer service function.

But if your type of business or chosen value proposition doesn't require high availability, it might be enough with "All questions are handled via e-mail (no phones)" and "All e-mails are answered within 24 hours".

Tip #73: Optimize customer service availability based on your value proposition

For unitedsurfcamps.com we had approximately one year of experimentation with high availability before we concluded to go for e-mails only with 24 hours' response. We did lose some sales on this, but the net effect was positive since time and effort could be minimized.

Just note that this can change over time since customer demands tend to increase and competitors are constantly improving. This means that if you make a valid trade-off between availability and cost today, there can become a hygienic demand in the future to increase your availability.

However, what is more important than the absolute availability is that you keep your promise. If you clearly communicate that all e-mails will be answered within 24 hours, most customers will accept this (even if many of them would prefer quicker answers). But if you don't keep the promise all affected customers will be irritated and give you bad reviews

Tip #74: Be clear with your availability and keep the promise

Once you have set the strategic direction of your customer service process you can focus on how to make it as cost efficient as possible (without affecting sales and customer experience negatively).

The first thing to consider is how you can "reduce" the questions your customers want to ask you by answering them proactively already in the sales funnel (as discussed in tip #51).

The second thing is to consider how you can answer the questions proactively just before they decide to contact you (e.g., via phone or e-mail). This can be done by channeling each questions via a "Frequently asked questions" (FAQ) section.

Tip #75: Channel each customer question via FAQ

As an example, this is what you will see when you click on "contact us" at unitedsurfcamps.com:

Ask us a question

Maybe you can find the answer in our FAQ section?

- Are there any age limits to go to the camps?
- Can I apply for a job at Unitedsurfcamps?
- Can I check availability and prices without making a reservation?

Full name:

E-mail:

Subject:

Which surf camp does your question regard: Algarve

Message:

The three questions being highlighted in the box are the most frequently asked questions we used to get via e-mail. By channeling the traffic via this top FAQ, we were able to reduce e-mail volumes by over 30%.

Just note that all questions cannot be "reduced." Sometimes customers want to ask you a question just to initiate a conversion to feel you are trustworthy. If they get a quick and trustworthy response, it will be the tipping point that makes them convert.

After working to reduce the questions to customer service, the next step is to answer the questions that must reach you in the most cost-effective and service-minded way.

If you read some management literature regarding Customer Service, you will hear about "first line" vs. "second line" customer service.

First line is the first person, to whom your phone call or e-mail is directed to. If this person cannot answer your question, it is redirected to the second line, who is an expert or process owner of the area your specific question is about.

When setting up the first line and second line structure, you want to use the pareto principle, meaning that typically 80% of the questions you receive are quite similar and should be answered by the first line. The remaining 20% are more complex, and it does not make sense to educate the first line to know all these details, hence it is better to redirect the customer to the second line.

Tip #76: Use the pareto principle to split the customer service into a first line and a second line

The first line typically consists of people working only with customer service, while the second line might have it only as part of the job. The second line might also be outside your company. For example, if you have outsourced logistics (tip #85) the second line for logistics questions would be your logistics provider. Same thing would be if you outsourced finance & accounting (tip # 91.)

Operating a customer service function can be quite costly, especially if you are located in a developed country with high labor costs. However in the global information society that we are living in, it is not obvious that your customer service function needs to be located in the same country that you are.

Business Process Outsourcing (BPO) has been a major trend the last decade, and today there are numerous options available to outsource your customer service to a BPO-provider in a low-cost country. For example, all customer service for unitedsurfcamps.com is managed from the Philippines, a country with people, who, on average, have excellent English skills and offer very competitive labor costs.

This kind of "offshoring" is not only limited to customer service. It can also be applied to web development and digital content management (discussed in Tip #88.) Basically you can be anywhere in the world and have "virtual assistants" located in a completely different place.

Tip #77: Use virtual assistants for first line customer service

The second largest cost after labor is the technology you use to answer questions. Phone calls can be quite an expense, for both you and your customers, if you handle them the traditional way. However, if you use voIP (voice over IP) providers such as Skype, you can conduct phone calls with a very limited cost and with high flexibility.

For example with unitedsurfcamps.com, we used to have different Skype-In numbers for all or largest markets. It means that a customer located in USA can call a USA-number, a customer in UK a UK number, a customer in Germany a German number, etc. This means that the customer only pays a small fee (as if he called a local number) while all calls end up in the same Skype account. This is available from Skype and other voIP-providers (such as Virtual Phone Line and Inphonex) at very affordable fees.[14]

For customers who have their own Skype account, they can even call you Skype to Skype at zero cost (for both you and the customer.)

---

[14] support.skype.com/en/category/ONLINE_NUMBER_SKYPEIN/

Tip #78: Minimize technical cost with using voIP (e.g. Skype)

For many customers it can be a big step to lift the phone and call customer service while shopping online. At the same time, they can feel that response time to an e-mail (directly or via "contact us" form) would be too long.

A smart way to balance this is to integrate a live chat widget on your website. The widget will show when somebody is online, and it is a very small, convenient step for the customer to start an interaction.

Tip #79: Use a live chat widget to enable high availability in a cost-effective way

Using a live chat widget can have a big impact on improving the conversion rates by "coaching" the customers through the sales funnel. However, it requires manpower (and hence cost and effort), so you need to compare the additional cost with the increased sales value you can receive.

The benefit of the live chat widget is that the same customer service person can have several conversions ongoing in parallel, meaning that it is typically more cost-effective than customer service via phone. The negative side is that it makes it easier for the customer to ask questions directly which otherwise would have been answered via your FAQ.

Integrating the chat widget is easy and not particularly expensive. There are many chat widgets (e.g., purechat.com) available in "freemium model", meaning that limited numbers of interactions per month are for free, but unlimited usage requires a subscription.

Something very important to have in mind is that all "customer service" does not occur within your controlled domain. In tip #33, we discussed that your Facebook page actually works as a parallel customer service channel and needs to be handled that way.

Additionally, your customers can say whatever they want in forums not controlled by you.

A classic example of this is the "Dell Hell" case study where a customer in 2005 got irritated with Dell's poor customer service and started blogging about it under the title "Dell Hell." When other customers, who had similar experiences followed, the results were a lot of traffic and links to this blog so when you searched for "Dell" on Google, the "Dell Hell"-warning would come up on Google's Top10 result. Eventually Dell made a total U-turn and is today a leading enterprise when it comes to customer engagements[15].

The key learnings here are that you need to handle customer service inside and outside of your domain. By regularly googling your company name or using services such as Google Alert or mention.com, you will find things being said about you on the Internet. You can handle these in a professional manner and be present and answer all questions openly and immediately.

Tip #80: Proactively check and handle what people write about you outside your site

In summary, the customer service process has many savings opportunities. But what is most important is that you are successful to keep customers happy by being proactive and keeping your promises.

---

[15] Further reading on the case: slideshare.net/chaturvedibraj/dell-hell-a-social-media-learning

Sourcing, Production & Transport

In a typical income statement, the first cost stated after the revenue is the COGS, meaning "Cost Of Goods Sold." If you are in the retail business, this refers to the goods you buy from your suppliers and you later resell to your customers. If your business has a production component, this is the cost of the raw material you need to source for producing the products you sell.

If you sell physical products such as shoes, books, clothes, food online, this will be a major cost for you. But on the other hand, if you enter an online business that sells digital products, you can eliminate this cost to a large extent.

For example, if you sell story books for children (in traditional format), you would first purchase the books, then keep them in stock, and then send them to your customers. If you instead sell the books in digital format (as in an e-book, application or a voice-book), your customers can download them directly from your website after check-out. The same rules apply for selling leads or services. If you can avoid sourcing, production and transport of physical products, you can also avoid a lot of extra work.

When we started unitedsurfcamps.com in 2005, we had a long list of business ideas we were considering to try. One of the reasons that we chose to sell surf trips was that it did not include any production and delivery of physical products; hence, we avoided a lot of hassle.

Tip #81: Consider to avoid production costs by selling digital products & services

This is of course mainly applicable if you are in the start-up phase. If you have an established company selling physical products, it is probably not something you should stop with. But maybe some of your products could be "digitalized" and sold in different formats to your customers?

If you do sell physical products online, there are still many best practices to keep the costs down. One important choice is which main tactic you use in the sourcing and production: "make to stock" or "make to order."

Traditionally, companies tend to use "make to stock." Meaning that they keep (sourced or produced products) in a warehouse from where the goods are sent to the customer. This is usually good for availability of the product, but it drives a lot of costs and risks:

✓ Cost of the storage room
✓ Cost of the storage personnel
✓ Cost of capital tied up
✓ Risk of damage of goods
✓ Risk of "out of stock", meaning the customer doesn't receive goods on time
✓ Risk of additional transport cost due to order split

The opposite of "make to stock" is "make to order." This means that you do not order or produce the product before the customer actually orders it from you (and has paid for it.)

In this scenario, you can avoid the costs and risks above and you get a fantastic way of free financing, since you get paid by a customer before you drive any cost.

Tip #82: Use "make to order" rather than "make to stock"

So how does "make to order" work practically? If we use the example of selling children books, you would not print the book before the order was made. A decade ago this was not possible, but with today's technology you can print in small series (even just one book) at a very low cost. With the rise of 3D-printing, you can even do it for more advanced products, like jewelry, accessories and technical components.

The down-side of "make to order" is that it often implies longer delivery times than if you have a product in stock, ready for delivery. One way to get around this is to digitally integrate your e-commerce system with your suppliers and send the purchased products directly from them, without you actually touching them.

Tip #83: Send directly from your suppliers to your customers

This is called "drop-shipping" and works best for businesses where the customers tend to buy only a few different products at the same time. If the typical purchase pattern is that your customer orders 20 different products from 10 of your different suppliers, it will not be acceptable for him to receive 10 different deliveries.

A middle-way is to keep your most common products in stock but source rare products directly from your suppliers. You can then choose either to split the order or to connect them at your warehouse before sending them as one batch to your customer.

"Make to order" is also optimal for customized products. For example if you design and order a tailor made shirt online via tailorcut.com, it is being produced according to your directions and sent directly from the tailor in Thailand, without passing any warehouse owned by tailorcut.com.

This leads us to another best practice, to source your products from developing countries with lower labor costs.

Tip #84: Consider sourcing from developing countries

Just keep in mind that sourcing from developing county can also increase the complexity of your business. Delivery times can be longer, it can be more complex to return faulty products and there is a risk that products get stuck in customs.

Having the above in mind, it is important to find trustworthy suppliers who are committed to the delivery times you agree on and who are flexible enough to help solve any problems that might occur.

Once the physical product is ready, either in your own warehouse or at your supplier, it is time to deliver it to the customer. Doing this on your own requires lots of resources in the form of transport means (e.g., trucks) and personnel. It is typically smarter that you outsource this to a third party logistics provider.

Tip #85: Fully outsource the logistics

If you are servicing only one or a few particular countries, you can find logistics companies who can handle the whole order fulfilment process for you. This means that the logistics company will do everything from the storing, order picking, and packing to transporting the goods to your customers. Many logistic companies also offer the reverse process with the claims reception and returning faulty products.

If you are planning to serve a global market, your best bet is to solve the transport service with a global company like DHL, UPS or TNT. They can also handle the whole logistics (also including warehousing, order handling and returns) on a global market, but it requires a larger scale.

One thing to consider if you are sending products cross-borders is to avoid having product trapped in customs. "Proper labeling" is key in this process. However, this aspect differs heavily between countries. Make sure to discuss potential shipping issues with your logistics partner before you start shipping, to avoid unnecessary costs and angry customers.

IT & Content Management

When starting an online company, one of the first practical questions you need to ask yourself is how your website will be developed and managed. Basically you have two extreme options:

1. Build and manage the website (including e-commerce platform) on your own
2. Buy a standardized hosted service

This is a very strategic question and depends on the logic and size of your business and your skills.

The first extreme – building the whole website on your own - is how I did it for unitedsurfcamps.com in 2005. This was possible by following many of the great tutorials about PHP web programming available online[16].

However, the first version of unitedsurfcamps.com was really crappy and was fully rebuilt in 2008 by a professional web designer. But starting on my own gave me invaluable insights regarding what can be done (and not) and how it all fits together. Even though I haven't written any code myself for years, I have great use of it when discussing and formulating requirements for web designers in various projects I have been involved in.

---

[16] e.g. codecademy.com/en/tracks/php

The other extreme is to use a full-service provider who will charge you a monthly fee for hosting your e-commerce. You can typically choose between a few different designs and get your logo and info placed where you want, but your have a very limited possibility to adapt the core structure of the system to your business model.

This model has been applied successfully by a friend of mine who is a passionate jewelry designer. She is using Tictail as a full-service provider for her site dagnyofsweden.com .

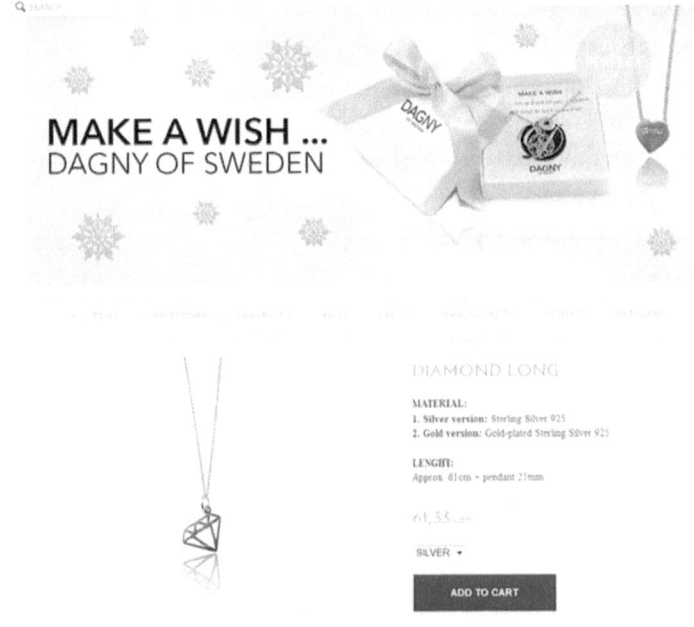

This full-service provided by Tictail only cost $3 per month and has saved her lots of hassle with the development and maintenance of her website. In the simplest format Tictail even offer a free of charge version of their system.

There is also a middle way in which you base your website on an "open source" e-commerce system (e.g., Magento.com), but you host it on your own and re-code it to fit your exact needs.

Tip #86: Make a strategic "build or buy" decision for your e-commerce system

There are several articles available online which compare different e-commerce platforms[17] and can give you further guidance in making this decision.

When building and developing your website, you also need to consider the labor cost of the web programmer. Doing the coding yourself is obviously the cheapest way, but maybe not the most sustainable.

The opposite is to use IT-consultants from large recognized enterprises, but they tend to charge very high fees, making them unsuitable for most small and medium sized businesses.

If you (or one of your co-workers) have some basic web-programming knowledge, it is quite easy to get this cost down drastically by using low cost web developers.

Tip #87: Consider using low cost labor for your web development needs

These low cost providers can be of two types. The first option is to use programmers from developing countries (e.g., India.) The downside to this option is that you will need to give very exact instructions, and you will inevitably run into some issues connected with languages and cultural differences.

---

[17] e.g udemy.com/blog/best-ecommerce-platform/

The second option is to use IT-students from your local market. They are typically quite eager to work hard at low cost (since they see it as a learning experience) and you won't experience problems related to neither language nor cultural differences. The downside can be that the students tend to move on to work for other companies than yours after their studies are completed and hence might not be able to offer a sustainable support to your business.

The code describing your website and e-commerce system also needs a "home," meaning a server where the data is stored. This can be completed on your own server(s), but is typically better to outsource to a web hosting provider.

There are five main things to consider when you choose web service provider:

1. Technology match - Your website is typically built either with ASP or PHP coding. The PHP host is for servers run on Linux while the ASP host is run on the Windows system. Make sure that your web host has the same technology that your website has.
2. E-commerce integration - If you are using a standardized e-commerce system (rather than building your own), it is good to check which web hosts the e-commerce system provider has the most positive experiences.
3. Server location - If you are running a local or national website, it is beneficial to have the server located in the same market to avoid traffic disturbances. If you are running a fully international website, the best solution is to work with a company that has multiple server halls around the world.
4. Capacity - The web host needs to have both storing space and bandwidth for your needs. If you are running a small business with a few thousand visitors per month, this is usually not an issue. But if the website you are trying to create is like a social

networking site with steaming videos, then you need more space and ability to scale fast.

5. Support - If your website is down, you want immediate and professional support to solve the issue.

The above things shall be balanced with the price you pay for the hosting, which is typically a fixed fee per month, depending on storage space and service quality.

Tip #88: Choose the right web-hosting for your needs

There are hundreds of web hosting companies available to choose from. Check out for example whoishostingthis.com/ to make a comparison.

Even if you buy a standardized full-service e-commerce solution, you will still need to handle most of the digital content creation and management on your own. Some of this will need to be handled by skilled web developers (as discussed above), but the majority is pure administration work. So let's now look into the best practices of effective administration.

Administration

All businesses require a certain amount of administration. Most of it is connected to monitoring and controlling the money streams in and out of the company, for example invoicing customers, paying suppliers and employees, managing accounting and tax declarations.

The good thing with an online business is that it is natural to automate as much of this as possible.

For example, a key enabler to minimize the administration with unitedsurfcamps.com is that we have built separate administration pages where our customers, partners and administrators can log in and manage the bookings and update information. By adapting this "back-bone" system to our needs, we have been able to eliminate approximately 70% of all time which was originally required to manage the business.

Tip #89: Automatize as much admin as possible

Another example is the money you owe your suppliers. Instead of them sending physical invoices to you, it is possible to automatize the money handling between you and them. Basically there are four options:

1. <u>Full integration</u> - Meaning that you code your systems to talk to each other automatically. This is the preferred option for suppliers most connected with your core offering (e.g., the one producing the goods you sell.)
2. <u>Automatic charging of credit card</u> - Meaning that you add your credit card number into your suppliers system which then automatically charges your card on a regular (e.g., monthly) basis. This is can be used with Google AdWords, Bing Ads and Facebook Ads.
3. <u>Direct debit</u> - Meaning that you give your bank approval to transfer money directly from your bank account to your supplier. The systems for direct debit vary between different countries, while the automatic charging of credit card is most favored by global suppliers.
4. <u>E-invoicing</u> - Meaning that your supplier sends the invoice in PDF to you (instead of in printed form.) You still have to manually pay the invoice.

Obviously, you cannot automatize all admin 100%. E.g., in the second example above you will still need to log in to Google AdWords, Bing

Ads and Facebook Ads to export the receipts of your paid service, to use in your bookkeeping. However, instead of doing this every time the transaction occurs, you can "batch" the administration work and complete many exports at the same time (e.g., once per month.)

Tip #90: Batch admin that cannot be automatized

The third way to get rid of admin is to outsource it, ideally to low cost labor.

As mentioned in tip #77, there exist numerous companies offering "shared service centers" for this in low cost countries.

Just remember that you can't outsource "your problems," meaning that you should first go through the two steps of automation and batching. After doing this a while, you can map and document the process so you will know exactly what it is you will be outsourcing. Then the key success factor is to write a very detailed (more detailed than you think) work manual for each process you plan to outsource.

Tip #91: Outsource admin once you know how to do it

Another important aspect is to agree in detail with the outsourcing provider how the work will be measured and paid for. This is usually documented in a "service level agreement" (SLA).

Summary

In summary there are numerous ways to minimize the costs and efforts of running an online business. The key principles for this are:

✓ Online business processes are easy to automatize, since it is "digital" from the start.

✓ The digital context also makes it easy to measure, compare and continuously trim the costs.

✓ Most things can be outsourced (customer service, IT, production, logistics, administration, etc.)

✓ But before outsourcing, you need to make a strategic decision about it and map the process.

How much focus you should put on the cost aspects of the business compared to revenue growth depends mainly on your business concept and funding.

If you have received seed capital for a business idea with the potential of being "the next Facebook," it is probably extremely crucial to focus on growth rather than cost and effort. You want to grow your member base in quick speed to secure the position of being the number one player. Even if your customers are not actually generating any income at the moment and/or your server capacity costs are escalating, these aspects can be temporarily ignored if you have a second phase plan where you will be able to capitalize even so.

However, when I founded unitedsurfcamps.com, I did it basically on a shoestring and the main purpose was never to take it to the stock-market and cash-in. Rather, it was based on a passion for surfing and online business. Since we started in 2005, I have been able to work less than four hours per week. I actually followed and applied all the best practices discussed above. In these "actual work-hours," I do not count the numerous surf trips I have completed around the world (fully funded by the company) visiting our different surf camp partners and surfing the best waves on the planet. That is truly mixing business with pleasure.

Practical tips presented in this chapter:

Tip #71: Set up a regular marketing evaluation routine

Tip #72: Track and calculate cost per conversion for all media mix, not only online

Tip #73: Optimize customer service availability based on your value proposition

Tip #74: Be clear with your availability and keep the promise

Tip #75: Channel each customer question via FAQ

Tip #76: Use the pareto principle to split the customer service into a first line and a second line

Tip #77: Use virtual assistants for first line customer service

Tip #78: Minimize technical cost with using voIP (e.g., Skype)

Tip #79: Use a live chat widget to enable high availability in a cost-effective way

Tip #80: Proactively check and handle what people write about you outside your site

Tip #81: Consider to avoid production costs by selling digital products & services

Tip #82: Use "make to order" rather than "make to stock"

Tip #83: Send directly from your suppliers to your customers

Tip #84: Consider sourcing from developing countries

Tip #85: Fully outsource the logistics

Tip #86: Make a strategic "build or buy" decision for your e-commerce system

Tip #87: Consider using low cost labor for your web development needs

Tip #88: Choose the right web-hosting for your needs

Tip #89: Automatize as much admin as possible

Tip #90: Batch admin that cannot be automatized

Tip #91: Outsource remaining admin once you know how to do it

Resources mentioned in chapter 6

Customer Service / Feedback Monitoring

- ✓ **Voice over IP providers** (e.g., skype.com) - Services that allow you to have different phone numbers for each market even though all calls end up in one single account for you.
- ✓ **Chat widgets** (e.g., purechat.com) - Enable you to have live chat discussions with customers who visit your website.
- ✓ **Alerts whenever your webpage is mentioned** (google.com/alerts or mention.com) - Good for handling customer service outside of your domain as well as tracking your PR activities.

Web development / Hosting Services:

- ✓ **Web programming tutorials** (e.g., codecademy.com/en/tracks/php) - Will teach you the basics of web programming.

✓ **Full-service e-commerce systems** (e.g., tictail.com) - Quick and cheap way to get started without any own programming, however limited possibilities of adaptation

✓ **Open-source e-commerce systems** (e.g., Magento.com) - Host it on your own and re-code it to fit your exact needs.

✓ **Hosting comparison services** (e.g., whoishostingthis.com) - Service to compare the offering and performance of multiple hosting providers.

CHAPTER 7

Grow in new dimensions, once the concept is proven

Introduction - The five dimensions of growth

There is a classic management slogan saying, "Think big, start small."
It means that if you try out too many things at the same time, you
will be overwhelmed and get stuck in details. However, when your
first core concept is optimized, using the learnings in previous
chapters, and proven (i.e., you are making money with acceptable
effort) it is time to take the next step and grow in new dimensions.

There are basically five dimensions which you can expand your
original business model into:

1. New Offerings
2. New Customer Segments
3. New Sales Channels
4. New Markets
5. Sell the Know-how

New Offerings

By new offerings I mean that you offer more products and services to
the same customers as before.

For example if you are selling sports shoes online, you might have a few different categories, like:

1. Running shoes
2. Trekking shoes
3. Tennis shoes

If you add on another category of shoes such as football shoes, it is still a natural optimization of your core business model: selling affordable sports shoes online!

But if you expand with relative parallel offerings, like:

✓ Tennis rackets
✓ Footballs
✓ Etc.

You are taking a first step to grow in a new dimension.

Another step is to start offering relative services:

✓ Personal training
✓ Sport event tickets
✓ Etc.

This growth dimension is based on you knowing your customers very well and being able to offer them more and more things based on this relationship. We discussed this already briefly in chapter 5 as a way to maximize the value of your customer base.

As mentioned in chapter 5, tip #67, you don't necessarily need to expand by yourself, but instead do it via partners (selling leads.) If you take the first step with a partner (and it is very successful), you can then take a further step and do it on your own.

Adding new offerings to your website is a very natural growth path, but it has some pitfalls. There are a lot of bad examples out there of websites that have completely lost their heart and structure by having too many offerings in the same place. Instead of increasing the sale, this can dilute the trustworthiness and the sales funnel effectiveness, meaning that your conversion rates will drop.

If you have concluded that a new offering is the right growth path for you to prioritize, you need to make a strategic decision on how it should be integrated in your online hierarchy. If the new category is far off and makes your website appear to look "messy," it might be better to promote it under a separate website. This way you can keep a "clean" and trustworthy story around specific niches you are targeting with each website.

Tip #92: Make a strategic decision between creating a new category vs. a new website

The downside of having separate websites is that you need to optimize both the organic and inorganic search traffic for more than one website.

However, it does not necessarily mean more administration work to have separate websites for separate offerings. If you build your system smartly, you can separate the "front-end" from the "back-end" of the system. The "front-end" is everything that your customers see and interact with, which can look completely different and must be optimized for the specific offering. The "back-end" is the "engine" of your system, i.e, how products, orders and payments are stored in data-bases and how you can access a control panel to manage these.

Tip #93: Separate the "front-end" and the "back-end" to get synergies from different websites with similar business models

When you grow by adding more offerings, it is important to keep a "trial and error"-approach. Remember that if you decide to expand the offering in one direction, you will not know the results until you see how the customers respond. Adding on more and more offerings can also put you in a bad spiral of making your website too "messy."

It will require some discipline to analyze your offerings and remove products or even whole categories that don't add significant value. The best way to do this is to continuously evaluate your offering using the "Pareto Principle." This means that you rank your products (or categories) in a falling order based on their share of the total accumulated sales value they stand for.

For example, in the picture below you see the example that three shoe categories (Running, Indoor and Trekking) together stand for over 80% of the total sales. These are your "A-products" and should be top priority.

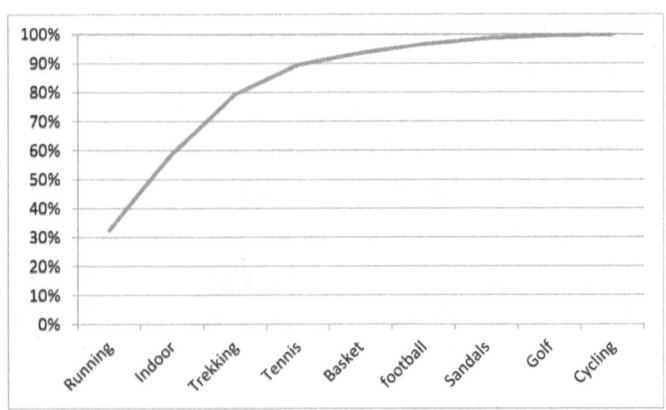

On the other side of the range, you see that Golf and Cycling shoes only stand for around 1% of the total sales. Hence, the question you need to ask yourself is if it is really worth to keep them? The customers of these kind of shoes maybe have a different purchase pattern than your typical customers? It would probably take a lot of time and effort to turn these categories into higher sales volumes. Probably you will get better "return on investment" if you focus your time and energy on driving up the categories that are already selling well?

Tip #94: Continuously pareto-evaluate your product line and "cut the tail" of non-value adders

Just note that sales volumes are not the only parameter. You also need to consider what margin you have on different product lines and how much effort they require to be properly managed.

Besides growing "horizontally", meaning that you add more categories in your offering, you can also work on the "service component" of the products you are already offering.

By doing this you should ask yourself what process steps your customers will go through to buy and use your product?

For example, if you are selling cufflinks online, it could be that many of your customers are buying these as gifts (especially just before Christmas). You can then offer to do the gift wrapping for them, for a small extra fee.

Tip #95: Offer enhanced services connected with your product

What kind of enhanced service you can offer depends on the kind of business you are in. Here are a few general examples to explore:

1. Customization - How can you make the product unique to your customer?
   a. Specific color?
   b. Printed name or initials?
   c. Customers making the design by themselves in your online store?
2. Prioritization - How can you offer your customer VIP treatment?
   a. Priority access to products on sale (before other customers?)
   b. Faster delivery of your goods?
3. Logistics - How can you make the delivery process more convenient?
   a. Help to carry goods into apartments and other destinations?
   b. Help mounting the product (e.g., if you are buying a furniture?)
   c. SMS notifications of delivery status?
4. Sustainability - How can you help your customer to be environmental friendly?
   a. Recycling of exchanged goods (e.g., if you buy a refrigerator?)
   b. Off-set the CO^2 emissions from the product/service?
5. Insurance - How can you reduce the risk for the customer?
   a. Money back in case product gets broken?
   b. Money back in case the service gets canceled or delayed?
6. Financing - How can you help your customer manage his cash flow?
   a. Not paying up front, but instead in the future?
   b. Leasing instead of buying a product from you?

The possibilities are endless!

New Customer Segments

The second dimension you can grow in is to offer the same products but to a different customer segment.

Customer segments can be "carved out" in different shapes and depend a lot on what kind of business you are doing. Here are a few variables that can be used to define customer segments:

1. Legal entity - The difference of doing business with consumers (B2C) or business with other companies (B2B). Other entities are organizations and governmental/municipal bodies.
2. Industry segment - Valid for B2B. The industry segment your potential customers are working in (e.g., production, retail, hotels, restaurants, hair dressers.)
3. Demographics - Valid for B2C. For example gender, age, nationality or place of living.
4. Interests – For example sports, IT, cars.
5. Spending willingness – Customers seeking budget deals vs. premium offers.

Let's say that you are selling gardening tools to private people who own their own houses (B2C). But you notice that a percentage of your customers are actually "professional gardeners" (B2B). There could be an "untapped potential" to split your offerings in two, to come closer to the specific needs of each segment.

For example, the professional gardeners would not want to see your prices including VAT, and it could be a "knock-out" criteria for them if they could just get an invoice and pay later instead of paying up front. The professional gardeners will also use your tools much more frequently than the private people since they are serving multiple houses and hence, could be interested in more advanced services, like maintenance service or leasing.

To service different customer segments online, you need to make a strategic decision if you should have a separate or common sales funnel for them.

There are basically three levels of this:

1. <u>Same Sales funnel</u> - Only small adaptations completed based on customers' input (e.g., showing prices including VAT for private people and excluding VAT for companies).
2. <u>Separate front doors</u> - Already at the top-domain, ask the customer which segment he belongs to. The rest of the interaction will be done in separate sales funnels optimized for each segment (but on the same website).
3. <u>Separate websites</u> - Different websites (and potentially brand names) for different segments. Remember that it is only the "front-end" that needs to differ. The "back-end" can be the same.

For example, the third option was chosen by my friend who designs jewelry. After some testing, she concluded it was better to have two different websites: <u>dagnyofsweden.com</u> focused on female customers and <u>wristofrocks.com</u> focused on male customers. Even though the "front-ends" (including the brand names) are separated, she still uses the same "back-end" system to service the customers.

<u>Tip #96: Make a strategic decision to have separate funnels or separate websites for new customer segments</u>

Another example is the budget vs. premium offers. If you for example are selling some type of clothes or accessories you would most likely come across one segment who is only interested in premium products (high quality, status and price), while another segment is only interested in budget products (decent quality to low price). To mix offerings to both these segments on the same website will most likely be confusing for both segments (and drive down total conversion rate). If you can have two different websites you could serve both segments successfully.

When you start serving multiple customer segments, it is important that you review and adapt your marketing as well. You need to ask yourself

✓ How can I reach this specific customer segment in the best way?
✓ What messages will specifically catch their attention?
✓ How can I make sure that each segment is presented the right message (and not one directed to another segment?)

You will solve part of this on a "keyword level" since specific keywords can be pointed to one segment. Part of this will be solved on the "marketing channel" level, meaning that you, for example, only advertise your B2B-offer on company forums, or your premium-offer in premium magazines.

Tip #97: Adapt the marketing to the customer segmentation (not the other way around)

New Sales Channels

E-commerce is one type of "sales-channel". Other sales-channels are:

1. Outlets - A physical place (e.g., a retail store) where the customers come to buy the products
2. Sales meetings - When a seller and a customer meet to discuss a business opportunity, it can either be a pre-booked or spontaneous meeting (e.g., somebody stopping you on the street.)

3. <u>Phone sales</u> - When somebody calls you from a call-center and offers you a deal. Or the opposite when the customers call a company to buy something
4. <u>Mail-order</u> - When you receive a letter that you respond to with an order confirmation. This is a sales channel which has shrunken dramatically with the rise of e-commerce.

These are all examples of traditional "offline" sales channels. Many e-commerce companies start in an offline sales channel and then expand into e-commerce, with the same offerings.

But you can also go the other way around. Meaning that when your fully online concept is proven you can expand into "offline" channels. This is a growing trend for many successful e-retailers[18].

To start your own outlets obviously requires lots of investments, but if you expand into the other offline sales channels, (meeting, phone, or mail) it can be done with limited costs.

Tip #98: Cross-sell between online and offline channels

Let's use the sport shoes example again. If you, for example, want to increase the sales of your football shoes segment, maybe one way is to expand into other sales channels? You could, for example, send a commercial mail to all junior football clubs in your region. Remember that each club probably has hundreds of children as members. In the mail campaign you offer large discounts for the whole team and offer to meet the team leaders to discuss this. You later follow this up with a phone call (referring back to the mail) and try to book a sales meeting. In the meeting, you bring your range of shoes and make an inspirational show engaging the junior players, while you convince

---

[18] shopify.com/blog/11884189-why-the-top-ecommerce-brands-are-moving-into-physical-retail-and-what-you-can-learn-from-them

the leaders and parents by proposing a discount. The next season you do the same (since children's feet grow fast), but you will then not need to do the actual phone call and visit. It should be enough that you send an e-mail with a specific discount code that can be used at your website.

Besides synergizing with offline sales channels you can also widen you online sales channels. This for example the case when you develop an application that customers can download and get a better shopping experience from smartphones and tablets. It is typically a bigger barrier to get your customers to download the app, but once downloaded you have fantastic direct sales channel set-up.

New Markets

The fourth growth dimension to consider is to expand your online offering to serve more geographical markets.

The most important thing to analyze is how attractive it would be for you to expand your business to a new geographical market. A brief market analysis should answer questions like:

✓ How big is the demand for your product/services on different markets?
✓ Is the demand growing or shrinking?
✓ How is the competition on the market?
✓ Are there any legal differences to consider?
✓ Is there any difference in how your product/service is consumed?

If you are not selling a physical product, this can be a quite simple step. For instance, with unitedsurfcamps.com we offered our services to a global audience already from the start. The key question for us has rather been whether we should adapt the website to different markets, meaning that you have different languages and maybe different domains (.de, .uk, .de, .fr etc.) or not?

This is a very strategic decision and depends on the business potential you see in the adaptation. So far we have chosen not to do this. There are many local competitors to unitedsurfcamps.com who focus on one market and language which we could win market shares from. But compared to other growth paths and our ambition to spend minimum time and effort on the business, it has so far been a no-go.

Tip #99: Make a strategic decision whether to adapt your website for different markets or not

If you choose to adapt your website, you can either adapt the whole system at the core, or you can use and adapt tools provided by Google[19].

If you are selling physical products, there are many more considerations to make. As we discussed under Sourcing, Production & Transports in chapter six, you need to have a logistics partner who handles international shipping, and you need to adapt to import rules so your products don't get stuck in customs. You also need to understand the taxation rules on your home market when you are exporting goods. For example, how the VAT should be handled differently within and outside EU or any other country you reside and do business?

---

[19] Check out developers.google.com/international/translation-tools for more info.

Sell the "Know-how"

Selling the "know-how" is the final dimension you can leverage from your original business idea. This is basically what I have done with this book, by documenting all my learnings from unitedsurfcamps.com and my network of friends in the online industry. If you enjoyed the book (and paid for it), I have succeeded ☺

Tip #100: Document your knowledge and consider if there is a different market or way to capitalize on it

Other ways to sell the know-how is to help other companies as a consultant, where you typically charge a fee per hour or a fixed fee for a certain project defined as a "deliverable." You can also sell know-how in the form of trainings and seminars or as being called in as a "field expert" and help other authors or consultants.

Summary

In summary, there are endless potentials to grow your business! But growth can also be a curse if you don't do it in a structured and thought-through way.

Before running out on a crusade to "conquer the world," I strongly recommend that you boil down your business idea to the simplest form and test it! If it works in the simplest form without any brand recognition and just buying some traffic from Google AdWords, it can be worth it to continue. If not, it is better to reset and try the next idea.

Once your concept is proven in its simplest form, you have a big potential in maximizing your profits by applying the best practices discussed in chapter 1-6 of this book. This is not a "one-time-thing" but rather a practice of "continuous improvements."

When you consider your core concept to be optimized at around 80%, you can make the strategic choice of new dimensions to grow. Remember Pareto and take note of the following!

1. New Offerings
2. New Customer Segments
3. New Sales Channels
4. New Markets
5. Sell the Know-how

Which dimension makes most sense for your business to pursue next?

Practical tips presented in this chapter:

Tip #92: Make a strategic decision between creating a new category vs. a new website

Tip #93: Separate the front-end and the back-end to get synergies from different websites with similar business model

Tip #94: Continuously pareto-evaluate your product line and "cut the tail" of non-value adders

Tip #95: Offer enhanced services connected with your product

Tip #96: Make a strategic decision of creating a separate funnel or separate website for new customer segments

Tip #97: Adapt the marketing to the customer segmentation (not the other way around)

Tip #98: Cross-sell between online and offline channels

Tip #99: Make a strategic decision whether to adapt your website for different markets or not

Tip #100: Document your knowledge and consider if there is a different market or way to capitalize on it

Final words

Have you decided to start an online business by now? In that case, I want to share with you a recommendation of immediate next steps to take. Following the below steps you should be able in less than 3 weeks to set up your own company and practically test your first choice of business concept in its simplest format.

Check list for first 3 weeks:

1. Start Google Adwords, Google Webmaster tools and Google Analytics accounts - After a few hours of tutorials, you are ready to practically test many of the tips in this book.
2. Do a brief market analysis to choose a business idea - See the recommended steps in the introduction chapter. Especially the part of using the key word tool in Google AdWords.
3. Draft the Business plan - Create a first draft of your business plan including the "elevator pitch" of your business idea and how you will make money using the practical tips in this book.
4. Decide website editor - First option is that you do it on your own with pre-defined templates in WordPress and/or by learning some basic web programming. Second option is that you find a friend or other resource that can build the first version of the website for you. Third option is that you start with a full-service e-commerce system such as tictail.com
5. Decide legal entity for your company - Different countries have different rules but usually it is very simple to register your own company. Once having the company registered, you can use the

company as the contract holder for the below points (instead of you as a private person.) Making business as a company also has lower risk and enables taxation benefits.

6. <u>Sign up for a web hotel</u> - Takes just a few minutes e.g., with <u>one.com</u> or similar provider.

7. <u>Register a domain name</u> - Can be done via your web hotel or, for example, <u>godaddy.com</u>

8. <u>Start a Bank account</u> - In the name of your company, make sure also to get a credit card.

9. <u>Choose a Payment service provider</u> - Use PayPal or DIBS and connect them to your bank accounts. If you use a full-service e-commerce system, this is already handled.

10. <u>Pilot the "core concept"</u> - Think Big but start small. Launch the simplest possible version of the website and just buy some small traffic volumes on Google AdWords. Is it already possible in this simplest form to gain more money on the traffic than what you pay to acquire it? If so, you have numerous opportunities to maximize the profits by applying the 100 tips in this book. If it does not work in the simplest form, it is better to reset and try the next idea.

Let's stay in touch

Thank you for reading this book, I hope you have enjoyed it. I truly hope that we stay in touch. I therefore encourage you to:

✓ Share any feedback you might have (good or bad).
✓ Share your successes / learning stories from your online business ventures online via your blogs, social media updates and elsewhere as well as directly with me via email and phone. I would be happy to promote your story (and link to you) from my website.

✓ Send me questions regarding your online business challenges. The answer may take few days, but I promise to get back to you!

You can reach me at:

The e-book page: onlinebusiness100.com
My e-mail: robert@onlinebusiness100.com

Good luck!
Robert